SPEED BUMPS
And Other Impediments to Life in the Fast Lane

VICKI PARIS GOODMAN

Copyright © 2025 Vicki Paris Goodman

All Rights Reserved. No part of this publication may be reproduced or transmitted in any form or by any means, mechanical or electronic, including photocopying and recording, or by any information storage and retrieval system, without permission in writing from the author or publisher (except by a reviewer, who may quote brief passages and/or show brief video clips in a review).

ISBN EBOOK: 978-1-64873-528-8
ISBN Paperback: 978-1-64873-527-1
ISBN Hardcover: 978-1-64873-532-5

Printed in the United States of America
Published by: Writers Publishing House
Prescott, AZ 86301

Cover and Interior Design by
Writers Publishing House

Dedication

Speed Bumps is dedicated to all the type A's of the world – those impatient, perfectionistic, obsessive and driven souls who know deep down there must be a better way.

Acknowledgements

Now I know why, when accepting their Oscars, actors and actresses gush with gratitude over those who helped steer them to stardom. No doubt these beloved mentors coached the now famous to avoid a multitude of hazards laying in wait to lead them astray.

Speed Bumps "dodged a bullet" thanks to my childhood friend Pam Husband, who read through numerous drafts until the book's purpose was well defined. Her scrutiny also uncovered several ambiguities and inconsistencies, and is responsible for my adding an entire chapter to the book. I am enormously grateful.

Many thanks to Pam's friend Rhe Vuer who, having never met me, read and reviewed *two* of the drafts. It is always a blessing to have the feedback of someone who doesn't know me nor my life story. Rhe's critique was invaluable.

My good friend Cheryl Williams listened patiently during many phone calls as I read her newly written excerpts from the book. Furthermore, I can always count on Cheryl to find any errors in punctuation, spelling and grammar, even as I pride myself on producing work containing none. Imagine my perfectionist's shame when she somehow discovered a few instances. My humiliation would have been far worse had these faux pas been exposed *after* the book's publication.

I so appreciate the efforts of Betsy Dennison, who read two drafts and provided detailed and helpful notes as to her impressions.

Psychology professional Gail Edgerton was able to evaluate the book's content from a clinical perspective to keep me from venturing too far afield with my layman's analysis of the type A personality.

Many thanks to my always supportive friend Jeannette Chiang Bardi, whose encouragement boosted my spirits during moments of self-doubt.

Much appreciation also goes to Beth Kreft and Mike McKeown for their wise commentary.

With gratitude I tip my hat to Angel Tuccy and Jamie Atkinson of NeedAGuest and Media Firestorm for their exceptional guidance.

I would be remiss if I failed to acknowledge the vital contributions of my loving parents, Muriel and Sheldon Paris, without which much of the raw material for *Speed Bumps* would not exist.

Finally, *Speed Bumps* would be hard-pressed to progress beyond the status of a PDF file without the expert assistance of Lizzy McNett.

Contents

DEDICATION..I
ACKNOWLEDGEMENTS II
PREFACE.. VII

PART I
Early Signs of Trouble

CHAPTER ONE...2
A Baseball Diamond Was a Girl's Best Friend
CHAPTER TWO...14
Bad Hair Days
CHAPTER THREE..27
The Awful Task of Shopping for Greeting Cards
CHAPTER FOUR 41
How Feminism Failed to Deliver

Part II
Obsessed

CHAPTER FIVE...72
Missed Opportunities and a Pickle Vendor
CHAPTER SIX...91
On Quasi-Perfectionism
CHAPTER SEVEN...127
Desperately Seeking Validation

PART III
Manifestations

CHAPTER EIGHT 162
Lessons Learned from an Intellectually "Impaired" Pet
CHAPTER NINE 176
Scenes from a Marriage
CHAPTER TEN 187
Ollalieberry (sp?) Madness
CHAPTER ELEVEN 199
Road Rage 101

EPILOGUE 211
AUTHOR'S BIO 217

Preface

Children are not things to be molded, but are people to be unfolded. – Jess Lair

Numerous books on personality types already exist. Many of them include analysis of the type A classification. But written by mental health professionals, they approach the topic from a strictly clinical point of view.

In writing *Speed Bumps*, I sought to speak solely from my own experience. My life's challenges were many, furnishing plenty of subject matter for the book's narrative. You will likely find this raw material at times admirable, often funny, sometimes heartbreaking, and occasionally shameful.

The stories told bare my soul to all who are willing to venture inside. I am an open book. (Furthermore, my self-deprecation appears to know no bounds.)

The human psyche isn't an exact science. Even if I were a psychology expert, it wouldn't be possible for me to attribute cause and effect with certainty. The exercise will always involve guesswork.

Still, I have had a lifetime to connect the dots, and certain hypotheses seem worthy of consideration. Case in point...

My otherwise loving mother, consciously or not, expected me to forego my own nature. Instead, I was to become her duplicate, her clone. To be fair, this was true only when it involved tastes, opinions and judgments of any kind. Add to this fact some unfortunate realities of my early physical appearance, and my burgeoning control issues seem inevitable.

Why the book's title? The type A is all about moving as fast as necessary to keep up. Falling behind causes our high-strung subject an unbearable degree of anxiety. But obstacles will always present themselves. *Speed Bumps* is all about those stumbling blocks in life, be they physical or psychological, that get in the way of the type A's relentless pursuit of her goals.

These goals range from objectives of vital importance to the utterly trivial. Examples might be:

- Staying caught up at work as tasks continue to mount
- Keeping her home in perfect order

- Ensuring her income tax return is prepared timely
- Getting through airport security when flying
- Seeking career advancement
- Resolving an issue with a service provider
- Completing her holiday shopping
- Finishing the reading of a book
- Arriving on time to a social engagement

As such, inconvenience and delays are intolerable "speed bumps" and the sworn enemy of the type A. They rob her of control, making her painfully aware of her vulnerability to external circumstances.

Everyone seems to have a different notion of what constitutes a type A personality. This likely stems from the clinical definitions varying so much from website to website, and in widely differing authoritative literature.

Still, I'm pretty certain I fit the profile, however "flexible" the attributes might be.

Since descriptions of the personality types have yet to be standardized, we remain happily unrestricted as to how we may portray them.

So, let's toss out a few of the available descriptive traits and, for good measure, dispense with the types C and D that make their way into some of the technical research, psychology books and online information.

Instead, let's go with simplified definitions, at least for purposes of this book.

Here is how I choose to define types A and B:

Type A

The type A is competitive, ambitious, proactive, driven, achievement-oriented and status-conscious. She is well-organized, likely due to her perceiving the practice to be a way to improve efficiency and speed in accomplishing tasks and goals. Hence, she is fast-paced and impatient, moving and working ever more frantically in response to her always heightened sense of urgency. She loathes delays and other forms of inconvenience, and is intolerant of others' hesitation and ambivalence since they often prolong the completion of a task or project. She is perfectionistic, likely as an adjunct to her competitive nature. The type A is assertive and sees little reason to avoid confrontation. However, confrontation carries the danger that her assertiveness will intensify into aggression, a reality she instinctively knows must be guarded against. In spite of her best efforts, she sometimes fails to avoid this escalation. The type A is especially prone to stress, perhaps even neuroses. As such, she is a control freak of the highest order.

Type B

The best way to understand the type B is to think of the individual as the polar opposite of the type A. She is relaxed and untroubled in almost every situation, and tends to be overly risk-averse. She avoids confrontation at all costs. The unshakable and well-centered souls among us are almost always examples of this type. The type B knows no urgency, accomplishing tasks at one steady and unhurried speed, regardless of deadlines. In a competitive situation, she focuses less on winning and more on experiencing the game or process. She is quite accepting of others, harboring few expectations for their attitudes and behavior. Whereas the type A often "manufactures" her own stress, the type B traverses life mostly stress-free. Occasionally, however, an outside influence over which she has no control (for instance, the behavioral excesses of a type A in her life) makes stress unavoidable.

The individual who is both type A and type B

My observations tell me most people possess hallmarks of both the A and B types. However, one type usually seems to dominate. On rare occasion, I have found a person blessed with approximately equal elements of both classifications. My friend Jeanine is an almost perfect example. She is highly motivated, well organized, detail-oriented, efficient, impulsive and assertive in an understated way. She is also patient, kind, self-disciplined and emotionally grounded. She tends to project a comforting effect onto those around her.

Jeanine is an uncommon blend we might call "AB." And her uniqueness goes a step further, as she exemplifies the *best* of A and B while displaying few of the negative traits comprising the two types. After all, type AB could also manifest as *any* balanced combination of A and B characteristics, including the problematic ones.

Types A and B in collaboration

Personal relationships, as well as work environments, almost certainly benefit from the participation of both personality types. The presence of a type B will serve as a calming influence on her type A counterpart. Conversely, the type A will push the safety-seeking type B toward greater life satisfaction, risk-taking and adventure by encouraging the gradual expansion of the seldom challenged "granite walls" securing the type B's comfort zone.

Speed Bumps is divided into three distinct sections:

Part I (Early Signs of Trouble) attempts to strike an evenhanded balance between my childhood's good times, of which there were many, and the considerable identity confusion emanating from my mother's suppression of my personal impressions and convictions. I was, in effect, denied a substantial portion of my own unique nature.

These opening chapters are intended to offer an in-depth probe into the possible causes of my controlling tendencies, which I believe spawned the type A impatience, perfectionism and drive gradually becoming my primary distinguishing characteristics. Various obsessions and compulsions "rounded out" the mix.

The type A reader can, perhaps, experience an "a-ha" moment when looking back on his or her own early life. Most likely some familial circumstance gave rise to the powerlessness and lack of personal authority preceding the inevitable grasping for control. A full-on type A personality makeup seems the only possible end result.

Part II (Obsessed) focuses on my working years, during which the aforementioned type A proclivities proved both highly beneficial and more than a little counterproductive.

This section's three chapters depict my fixations on fanatical neatness, inconsequential pet peeves and dating men of a particular "hazardous" kind. Ultimately, I went to ridiculous lengths to prove I could satisfy an admittedly arbitrary definition of career success.

Perhaps type A readers will have some "fun" meeting or exceeding the nonsensical nature of my obsessions by comparing them with their own. We type A's are so competitive!

Part III (Manifestations) delves into the inevitable results of motivations and traits difficult to attribute to anything other than the type A.

For example, I expected others to equal my personal brand of perfectionism. Consequently, I largely ignored the worthy aptitudes and skills those individuals brought to the table. A cat I adopted years ago taught me a valuable lesson about pre-judging someone based on one or two qualities alone.

My first marriage merited its own chapter for its depiction of an unsuccessful alliance of two *immature* type A individuals.

On a lighter note, I offer an example of how a type A might engage in fun. Yes, it's quirky by non-type A standards. In any case, you'll enjoy the read.

And then there is road rage. Need I say more?

I assure you, along the way I made sincere efforts to develop coping mechanisms. Few of them were successful.

Speed Bumps is intended to be wholly relatable. As such, it is important to recognize we type A's are not alone. I believe there are many who will identify, some so strongly the stories may bring them to tears. Offering myself as an example to which other type A's can emotionally connect is my primary reason for writing *Speed Bumps.*

As for the always laid-back type B's out there, I suspect many have type A's in their lives. These far more easygoing type

B souls are surely at a loss to understand the impulses and behaviors of their type A friends and loved ones.

Hence, my secondary purpose is to improve the outsider's knowledge of the "phenomenon" by highlighting my type A inclinations, how they have played out in real life, and what may have engendered them. In this way, I hope the type B can find ways to accommodate, perhaps even help, her type A's.

Note my choice of the word "help." This suggests the type A possesses a personality *disorder*, a condition in need of "fixing."

In fact, I do believe a type A personality exhibiting extreme or out-of-control behavior may benefit from intervention.

This is not to say there aren't highly advantageous aspects of the type A personality. Some of the most productive people I know, myself included, are type A's.

But impatience is rarely helpful. And the need to be in control often comes at the expense of teamwork, task delegation, peaceable relationships, and the enjoyment of common everyday pleasures. Indeed, a type A rarely "stops to smell the roses."

Throughout *Speed Bumps,* when speaking of the generic type A individual, I have employed the feminine pronouns "she" and "her." This was an arbitrary choice, not at all intended to imply that the book's narrative is more appropriate to women of the type A persuasion than to their male counterparts. The book is equally pertinent to type A's of both sexes.

So, do read on. I hope you will find these chapters both enlightening and entertaining. Please let my abundant self-deprecation not have been in vain!

Part I
Early Signs of Trouble

Chapter One
A Baseball Diamond Was a Girl's Best Friend

One of my first recollections of great success was playing baseball with the boys. – Linda McMahon

My baseball story is a particularly fond memory, though not without its "speed bumps," as you will see. Please accept its inclusion as a mostly happy childhood exploit and not related to anything particular of a type A nature. Perhaps view the tale as a counterbalance to the trials yet to befall me.

I was a tomboy. Do they still call it that?

To be precise, my friends were girls, but I had this other life Carol and Mindy knew nothing about and wouldn't have understood. This was unsurprising, as my two friends weren't saddled with curly hair, freckles and pointy glasses frames fitted with "coke bottle" lenses. At age ten, it was possible for them to go to school looking like girls. My lot was to wonder what that was like. So, I concentrated on getting good grades, practicing violin, and perfecting my mastery of a baseball glove.

It so happened my dad was a first-class all-around athlete. In college he'd excelled at football, baseball and swimming. Later on, he took up classic Brooklyn-style four-wall handball.

All you had to do was go watch one of Dad's handball matches at the "Hollywood Y" and you were effectively "transported" back to New York City, where men wore boxer shorts and athletic shirts, and had that manly gymnasium smell. The names on Dad's handball tournament trophies were all Jewish and Italian, and the best player of them all was named Stuffy Singer... But I digress.

Dad would come home from work wanting to play catch with a hardball and baseball gloves. My younger brother Bobby had eye muscle issues affecting his depth perception. This rendered him a mediocre player at best, especially when batting or fielding. Catching with a glove certainly wasn't ever going to figure in his skill set.

Consequently, Dad sought to mold me into his baseball throwing and catching protégé. And, if I may be so bold, I became good with a glove, *really* good.

The year was 1965 and little brother Bobby turned eight years old, old enough to join Little League. In spite of Bob's impaired depth perception, our family went to the try-outs and watched as the boys lined up and auditioned by batting, throwing, catching and running.

Bobby made one of the teams in the "farm league" – the training ground for future Little League sluggers. Dad volunteered to umpire at some of the games, while Mom signed up to periodically run the snack bar. And me? I sat in the stands getting hooked on the energy and atmosphere of the place.

Every game started out the same way. Piped in over the PA were the national anthem, followed by the Little League pledge. After the pledge came the "Little League song," forever branded on my brain:

"When the umpire calls and he hollers 'Play ball!' hear them yell 'C'mon Little Leaguer...'"

To this day, I whisper that song to myself every time I watch a baseball game.

If Dad wasn't umpiring at that night's game, he and I might throw the ball around. The prior Hannukah I'd received my first baseball glove. I got so good, the "minor league" boys in my class at school were noticing my talent during catching sessions with Dad at the Little League field. Their team had an unimpressive first baseman, and I have no doubt they were hoping for a replacement.

I bided my time the rest of the season and worked on taming my rather wild throwing arm. For some reason I had been unable to develop an accurate overhand. But while Dad and I were throwing the ball back and forth one day, he and I discovered I had a mean "sidearm" throw.

It featured a comfortable twist of the wrist. Best of all, it zeroed in on its target practically every time, veering a few centimeters off its mark only occasionally. Needless to say, Dad and I went with the sidearm. I was ready.

The next year, it was try-out day again. Dad was taking Bob who, now a year older, aspired to the minor league. I tagged along. Bobby made the desired cut.

I complained to Dad, "I wish they would let girls play so I could try out."

This is where a little understanding of my dad becomes necessary. Notwithstanding his athletic prowess and regular guy psyche, my dad was a little peculiar. Apart from sports, his favorite pastime was ignoring "NO TRESPASSING" signs.

A normal father would have responded to my yearning desire to try out, "Honey, I'm sorry. You know girls aren't allowed. You can throw the ball around with the boys after the game."

Not my dad. Normalcy wasn't his style.

Dad's response to me was a matter-of-fact, "So go get in line and try out."

"Really?!" I questioned Dad, in disbelief at his suggestion.

Although, knowing Dad, I shouldn't have been.

So, I stood in line, awaited my turn, and tried out.

Guess what? I made the team that had so badly lacked a competent first baseman the prior season. They still needed one.

The boys on my team were ecstatic. Since I looked like a little boy, the coach was none the wiser, and the boys weren't telling.

I happily began attending pre-season practices. I was living the dream, a dream come true.

It was the third week of pre-season practice, and I happened to be standing in earshot of our team's coach when one of the mothers, Mrs. Upton, walked by. She knew me, as her daughter was in my grade at school.

She innocently greeted me, "Hi, Vicki!"

The coach, having been led to believe my name was Vic, spun around to look my way. He suddenly appeared flustered, his eyes open wide, his face ashen.

The secret was out and the jig was up.

The boys came running in from the field, yelling, "Coach, let her play! Let her play!"

But Coach had no choice. Girls weren't allowed in Little League back then. It was against the rules. Coach would have to let his first baseman go.

My Little League career ended before the season officially started. I never even got to put on a uniform.

Once again relegated to the stands, I watched Bobby's games with interest. It had been discovered my bro' was a gifted pitcher. I was so glad he'd found his Little League niche in spite of his vision challenges.

My favorite games, however, were those in which Dad was the home plate umpire.

Other "umps" overdramatized the part, making a distinct coordinated hand and arm gesture as they loudly vocalized, "Steeee-rike!"

Perhaps as a result of the theatrics, they got their fair share of criticism for poor calls. Parents will be parents, even back then.

But nobody ever seemed to object to Dad's calls. He had an understated way of "umping." It was quiet and competent, and it inspired confidence. I was so proud.

I also took to helping Mom out in the snack stand. Favorite treats were the steamed pastrami sandwich on an onion roll, a big vinegary sour pickle, and the most excellent "frozen milkshake bar" – a candy bar similar to a Milky Way that someone had the good sense to put in the freezer. Frozen, the milkshake bar was ten times as chewy, at least ten times as good, and undoubtedly ten times as likely to loosen a filling or inlay. Not to mention, my temporomandibular joint is paying the price today. It's worth it.

As for Mrs. Upton, she may have inadvertently ended my Little League aspirations. But she gave me something far more valuable in the long run. A gift more consequential than being first baseman of the minor league team from which I'd been so unceremoniously ousted.

She gave me hope.

You see, Mrs. Upton was a very pretty woman.

One day she approached me at the Little League field and said, "Vicki, you know, I looked just like you when I was your age. Here, I brought a picture to show you."

Mrs. Upton produced a grainy, but still fairly clear, photo of herself at about age ten. She really had looked a lot like me!

Is it possible I might be pretty someday? Lovely-looking like Mrs. Upton?

The thought remained in the back of my mind as I faced what would be the significant challenges, and *pain*, of getting myself through the next three decades.

My ball playing travails remained largely at bay throughout my teenage years and young adulthood, except for a brief stint as the first baseman, and only female, on my employer's softball team.

Softball didn't quite do it for me. That big clumsy "mushy" ball just never felt as decisive landing in the pocket of my glove as a hardball had.

It wasn't until I turned forty and started dating my husband Sam that I once again had a reason to get the baseball glove "out of mothballs." I believe it was our second date when

Sam mentioned something about enjoying playing baseball catch. I couldn't resist suggesting we throw the ball around sometime.

I remember Sam called it "having a catch." I found his east coast phrasing endearing.

On our next date, we had located the gloves and a ball and went about the task of finding a suitable spot for the experiment. A few blocks from my house there was a nice shady park, not too crowded with picnickers.

We started with a series of well-controlled volleys. Observing I was perfectly comfortable, and a little bored, with the level of play, Sam began to throw harder.

It didn't take long for him to ask, "Do you ever *miss* one?"

"Not really," I sheepishly answered. "Not unless it's thrown so wild I can't get to it by running or jumping."

"Wow," he must have said.

Sam became fond of telling people I never missed.

Well, the old glove was in pretty bad shape, the laces cracking and breaking, and the pocket woefully scuffed up and thinning in places. I think it was a Wilson.

I'd always secretly wanted a Rawlings. So, for my birthday the following year, Sam presented me with a brand new, jet-black Rawlings glove.

My turn to say, "Wow!"

I felt like a thirteen-year-old again.

The Rawlings took a long time to "break in." The stiff new leather would eject the ball as I grasped upon impact. And the tendonitis in Sam's shoulder prevented us from working out the gloves very often. It took a few years, but the Rawlings at long last softened up.

Thinking back, I feel a little sorry for my junior high school friend Chloe. I had my glove with me one day when I'd been invited over to her house. She announced to her mom she was going to get a baseball glove so I could show her how to catch.

With me standing there, Chloe's mom proclaimed, "No daughter of mine will ever own a baseball glove!"

This was one of several instances while growing up in which I was made to feel like a very poor excuse for a girl.

Like my Little League career, Chloe's baseball chapter ended before it began. In spite of the tough time I endured awaiting late-blooming womanhood, I'm glad I had a baseball chapter. I'll bet Dad's glad, too.

Chapter Two
Bad Hair Days

It sometimes happens that a woman is handsomer at twenty-nine than she was ten years before. – Jane Austen

A girl's appearance can be a source of great disappointment, a "speed bump" leading to tremendous unhappiness and angst. In elementary school and beyond, most of us want little more than to simply fit in. This is true even if it means being unextraordinary in any way. If given the chance, a school-age girl would sell her soul to look like everyone else.

I suppose almost every child has her cross to bear. Mine was my hair. And the hair I was born with had me wondering by age nine what I'd done to make the responsible party (God? my parents?) so angry with me.

Was my hair a "speed bump" on the road to adulthood? Absolutely it was. And, apart from a brief respite in high school, my disastrous head of hair continued to impede my progress toward self-acceptance well into my 40s.

My hair was a thick coarse black mass of curls differentiating me from the other girls in school in a way no child wishes to be set apart. Curls were one thing. But the coarseness, with each strand's thickness easily visible to the naked eye, was a physical characteristic no little girl should have to abide.

You see, my hair never hung. It never flowed nor swung. It just sort of stuck out, resisting all efforts to manage it into a workable coif capable of making its host feel the least bit attractive.

As I grew older, I frequently wondered what unique and ill-fated combination of my parents' genetics could have produced my hair. My mother had average looks, and Dad was dreamboat handsome. The hand I'd been dealt was beyond unfair. It proved a relentless and daily bummer.

Even my brother Bobby had relatively straight hair when we were young. It got curly later on. But boys could wear their hair buzz-cut short, or even long and scraggly once the 1960s and 1970s made uncontrolled hair ever-so-chic.

The texture of boys' hair just didn't matter as much as the feel and look of girls' hair. Hence, like most kids, and unlike his sister, Bobby was no freak.

Heck, I just wanted to blend in. Was it too much to ask to have a chance to be minimally fetching by the time I reached junior high school?

Even the girls with stringy thin hair were objects of my envy. At least they were normal. Perhaps those girls were not striking in any way, but they would never be called "ugly." More on that later.

Suffice it to say, I was convinced I was repulsive, and no amount of my mother gushing over how adorable she thought I was could change my mind.

Mom dutifully took me to various beauticians for haircuts, each one representing a fresh possibility that I would be transformed into someone pretty, or cute, or at least passably average-looking. Each time my hopes were dashed. Every new haircut was as disappointing as the last.

I had to face reality. No one knew what to do with my hair. And I feared no one ever would.

I experienced a glimmer of hope one Saturday when my friend Terry's mother announced she would chemically straighten my hair. I thought I'd struck the mother lode. I willingly submitted to the procedure, excited to see what I would look like with ordinary hair.

Well, I got my wish. Using the mirror handed to me when my newly straightened hair was done processing, I marveled at how normal I appeared. For the very first time, I saw new possibilities for a promising future. I would finally be like the other kids in school. Heck, I might even get boys to like me.

Well, wouldn't you know it? I had twenty minutes of bliss, at which point my hair suddenly began to coil back up like a piece of stretched out curly ribbon after the scotch tape forcing it straight gives way due to adhesive failure.

In elementary school things weren't as bad as they might have been. The saving grace was my best friend Carol, a good-looking redhead who was quite popular. Her friendship shielded me from the lesser "angels" among our classmates.

My being one of the better students in our grade also seemed to make a positive difference. These facts earned me a modicum of respect and saved me from being taunted as was Dora, the most socially unfortunate girl in our class.

Poor Dora was overweight, an average student at best and well known for bringing lunches to school the other kids found disgusting. Dora was treated badly beyond words and my heart went out to her each and every day.

I refused to participate in the "sport" of humiliating Dora, not due to a similarity of our circumstances, but because I wasn't a mean kid. If only I'd been prettier and more popular, I might have been in a position to fend off the worst of the ridicule directed at Dora. My fantasy was that she might have been spared years of abuse.

As one of the more attractive girls, I would have befriended Dora, or at least pretended to like her, endowing her with my seal of approval. The other kids would have had no choice but to leave her alone.

This brings to mind a heartbreaking episode from a Saturday afternoon when I was about eleven. I was walking with Carol, Mindy, and another friend Effy. The four of us were headed from the bowling alley, where we spent every Saturday morning, to the heart of Studio City's main commercial district.

My three girlfriends lived in an upscale neighborhood in the hills off Laurel Canyon Blvd. Their parents had enrolled them in the Saturday league at the local bowling alley. Of course, I wanted to join the bowling league, too.

My parents, who were less well off, and were already footing the bill for my weekly violin lessons, gave me a choice between bowling and violin. I stuck with violin.

I rightly reasoned my friends would be happy to have me join them at the bowling alley on Saturdays, regardless of my status as a bowler. Instead, I would learn bowling's unique and, in my estimation, *fascinating* scoring system. It would cost Mom and Dad nothing if I tagged along and volunteered to keep score instead of participating as a bowler in the league. (This was years before automatic scoring was installed in bowling alleys. It makes me smile to reminisce about the "good old days" when I scored my friends' bowling matches by hand.)

On this particular Saturday, as we strolled from the bowling alley along Ventura Blvd., we decided to alter our usual route. Instead of trekking past the shops on Ventura, we ambled through a quiet neighborhood on a street paralleling the boulevard. We passed a house where a pretty 40-ish blonde woman was tending to the garden in her front yard.

Smiling, she addressed us with a cheerful, pleasing voice, "Hello girls. I believe you are classmates of my daughter."

Our curiosity piqued, I asked, "Who is your daughter?"

The lady proudly replied, "Dora."

Stunned, we acknowledged we did indeed know Dora.

I will never forget the lump in my throat, and the ache in my heart, as we overcame our shock sufficiently to bid Dora's mother a friendly goodbye. As I write about the incident, tears stream down my face.

The hush that overcame four chatty, giggly pre-teen girls as we continued our walk down Dora's street spoke volumes.

It struck me like a bolt of lightning: Dora's mother seemed completely unaware of the cruelty her daughter endured at school day in and day out.

Is it possible Dora suffered all those years in silence, never once seeking the counsel and reassurance of her own mother? Did she do it to spare her mother the pain the knowledge of her daughter's terrible treatment would inflict? Could an eleven-year-old Dora possess such rare strength of character? Or was Dora so ashamed of her bullying at the hands of her classmates she'd given herself no choice other than to keep the awful secret?

I have no idea what became of Dora. But I hope she blossomed and is enjoying a happy life with a loving husband.

Dora's story is a bit of a digression. But it's a worthy one, don't you think?

Soon afterwards Carol, Mindy, Effy and I, and all the other kids in our class, went off to junior high school. My excitement was over the top. For one thing, I was one of two kids out of the entire area's sixth grade graduating classes to have successfully auditioned and been accepted into our new school's advanced orchestra. I also had a wonderful new wardrobe of adorable skirts and dresses, mostly made by my grandmother, all with matching shoes and fishnet stockings. As such, my regrettable coarse black curls drifted a bit further from my mind.

They receded into the background, that is, until one day when I made my way to class, and an unfamiliar boy passed me in the hallway. We made eye contact before proceeding past each other.

Looking straight at me while craning his neck for full effect, he loudly opined, "You're ugly!"

It happened just that way.

Things improved substantially in high school thanks to a fad hairstyle called the "afro," which was suddenly acceptable regardless of the wearer's skin color. Added to this well-timed fact was one other little detail...

I'd been complaining about my eyeglasses, as I was no longer seeing well at a distance. Mom and I paid a visit to the optometrist.

After testing my vision, the doctor asked Mom how old I was.

Mom answered, "Fourteen."

"Is she especially responsible? Most fourteen-year-olds aren't particularly," the doc continued.

I recall feeling a little self-conscious being present while Mom and the doctor were talking about me as though I weren't in the room.

"She's *unbelievably* responsible," Mom confidently stated, which puffed up my ego a bit.

"Good," said the doc, "because your daughter needs contact lenses. She has such extreme nearsightedness that the space between her glasses lenses and her eyes is causing a significant amount of strain. At her age excessive strain causes the myopia to progress rapidly. We usually don't prescribe contacts for patients under sixteen. But we'll go ahead and make an exception in Vicki's case."

A couple of weeks later, I received my contact lenses. After having some initial trouble getting them into my eyes, I finally got the hang of it. I will never forget the first day I wore them to school.

It was early morning, and I was on my way to my first period class in the main building. A boy I didn't know was walking in the opposite direction.

He startled me by calling out, "Hey!"

I stopped and looked over at him while his gaze was glued to my face.

He said, "You're actually kinda cute!"

He was on his way before I had a chance to reply.

The "elongated afro" I'd settled on for my hairstyle, along with the contact lenses, had made all the difference in my appearance, and also my self-confidence. Everything changed, that is, until I went off to college. More on that later.

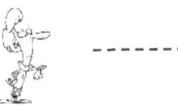

I acknowledge everyone has bad hair days. The thing is – apart from my three years sporting an afro in high school – it wasn't until my early 40s before I had a *good* one.

Enter Sam's cousin Sybil, who happened to be a hairdresser. When Sam was due for a haircut, we would drive about 45 miles from my home in Long Beach all the way to the west San Fernando Valley so Sybil could cut Sam's hair.

On one of these weekend excursions, as Sybil snipped away at Sam's silver locks, the owner of the shop walked in. He and I chatted for a while, and I made an offhand remark about my unfortunate hair.

Without missing a beat, he suggested, "Oh, have Sybil cut it. I mean it. Have her cut your hair."

"Really?" I asked, seeking any reason at all to believe I might be pleasantly surprised if I entrusted my coarse curls to Sybil.

"Yes! Sybil's a *wizard*. I'm telling you she'll do something fabulous," he assured me.

I called out from across the room, "Sybil, do you want to cut my hair when you finish Sam's?"

"Sure," replied Sybil. "I can do that."

And she did.

As a result, we got to Sybil's favorite sushi place almost an hour later than usual. And I happily consumed my Kamikaze Roll while flaunting the second haircut I ever really liked.

Chapter Three
The Awful Task of Shopping for Greeting Cards

"People tend to raise the child inside of them rather than the child in front of them." – Joe Newman

Perhaps this chapter says more about my wonderful maternal grandparents than it says about how much I hated buying a greeting card for Mom or Dad. So be it. Still, I believe the story is instructive, constituting a "speed bump" of particular significance.

When I was younger, buying a greeting card for Grandma or Grandpa was easy. They were wonderful, loving, inspiring people, and the sentiments in the grandparent cards at the store always suited them to a tee. The schmaltzier the better – it all applied.

I loved being with Grandma and Grandpa. It was a pleasure to choose their Mother's Day, Father's Day and birthday cards. Doing so seemed a natural result of our perfectly effortless grandparent-grandchild relationship.

Grandpa had no undesirable qualities, as far as I could tell. He was affectionate, generous, unselfish, loyal, and had a good sense of humor. Grandpa fixed our bicycles and roller skates, and assembled new toys we'd received for birthdays and Hannukah.

He hated it when one of his grandchildren spent his or her allowance on a present for him. To convince us not to buy him a gift, he even claimed to dislike the chocolate-covered ginger candies we knew he loved.

Grandpa adored fruit. He made almost daily runs to the produce sections of various supermarkets to buy the best fresh specimens at the lowest prices. In his charming Yiddish accent, Grandpa would lovingly describe the items he'd just purchased as he shepherded me into the kitchen to share in his latest acquisition of "beautiful nectarines" or "delicious plums."

Dried peaches, apricots and pears were other favorites one could find in copious quantities in Grandma and Grandpa's pantry. Of their four grandchildren, I was the one to have inherited Grandpa's love of fruit.

Grandpa and I shared an affinity for other foods, as well. Although Grandpa died many years ago, from time to time I will still indulge in a fabulous concoction of diced Kosher pickles mixed with sour cream. I'm pretty sure it was Grandpa who invented this taste sensation, and I was a devotee from the start. Fortunately, I was blessed with normal blood pressure, as a big bowl full of pickles and sour cream probably contains as much sodium as a dozen salt-rimmed Margarita glasses.

I recall watching Grandpa "put up" a batch of cherry schnapps when I was about ten years old. I asked Grandpa when it would be ready to drink.

My eyes must have bugged out when he replied, "About twenty years."

Of course, that was an endless amount of time to a child my age. And every year or so, I would ask Grandpa how the cherry schnapps was doing. He said he'd taste it for the first time when ten years had passed.

Sure enough, when I turned twenty, Grandpa pulled out the schnapps for its first tasting. And when I was about thirty, he proclaimed it was ready to drink. It was far too strong for me and the rest of the family, so the schnapps was mostly enjoyed by Grandpa… and Grandpa alone.

Grandma was the character of the two. She was a pretty little old lady with a wonderful smile and sparkling eyes. She made outstanding chopped liver and the best cabbage borscht ever. The peppery gefilte fish she tirelessly prepared for Passover couldn't be beat. She and Grandpa would grind three different kinds of fish to make it wholly authentic.

Her luxion (noodle) kugel was the only savory version I've ever had. Everyone else's grandma sweetened it, many also adding raisins. By comparison, Grandma's was a marvel of buttery, cheesy goodness.

Grandma always prepared way too much food. So, I was surprised one evening when she'd invited me over to have oxtails. I was about twenty-five at the time.

Grandma knew Grandpa and I were both fans of oxtails, a dish wholly rejected by the rest of the family. When I arrived, I was quite taken aback by the relatively small amount of food on the stove. It didn't even look like enough for the three of us. Soon I found out why.

You see, Grandma had a thing for junk food that closely matched Grandpa's devotion to fruit. Before serving up the oxtails, Grandma admitted she'd been yearning all day for a Big Mac and French fries. She asked if I wouldn't mind going to the McDonald's down the street to pick up a burger and fries. By the time I returned, dinner would be ready. I was happy to make the trip to retrieve Grandma's fast food.

As it turned out, Grandma spent the last ten to fifteen years of her life eating little more than Fritos and Snickers bars.

As she was in her late-80's and losing weight, we didn't fight it. We figured it was better than her eating nothing at all.

Grandma sewed many of my dresses as I grew up. She also made wonderful little outfits for my Tammy and "Poor Pitiful Pearl" dolls, and for my cousin's Barbie.

Aside from being the very example of domesticity, Grandma had another life, as well. Back in the day, and throughout my childhood years, she was a small-time political activist for what I suspect were radical causes.

There were numerous photographs on the hallway walls in Grandma and Grandpa's modest Fairfax-area apartment. Many of them depicted Grandma the activist. One showed her shaking the hand of ex-football star Rosey Grier at a political event. Another frame hanging on the same wall displayed a letter to Grandma signed by none other than President John F. Kennedy.

Whenever we visited, Grandma and Grandpa would send my family home with a freezer load of our favorite foods. There would be spinach borscht, beet borscht, the universally-loved cabbage borscht and Grandma's soup concoctions, always packaged neatly in recycled quart or half-gallon milk cartons sealed shut with masking tape.

If Grandma had recently made her half dollar-size meat or potato knishes, or her chocolate-frosted banana cake, ample portions of those would also be packed to go. And Grandpa could usually be counted on to stealthily include little fresh fruit treasures – "lovely peaches" or "wonderful sweet pears" – that we might not discover until we got home and unpacked the bags.

I also remember these funny little ice cream drinks in glasses with silver and blue fish painted on them. Whenever we visited, Grandma and Grandpa would always ask us grandchildren if we wanted a "soda," my grandparents' imprecise name for a float. These were any soft drink with a scoop of some flavor of ice cream tossed in. Purist that I am, I would generally pass unless my grandparents happened to have root beer on hand.

Much later, Mom told me something about Grandma and Grandpa I almost wish she'd kept to herself. I say *almost* because I believe the truth should virtually always be exposed to light. But the anecdote, constituting another "speed bump" on my road through life, makes me sad every time I think of it.

Mom told me Grandpa used to bring Grandma flowers every Friday afternoon when he arrived home from work. I was charmed by the sweetness of this fact until Mom told me why

Grandpa ended the practice. I was shocked to learn Grandma had had a brief affair with a family friend. According to Mom, after Grandpa found out about the affair, he never brought Grandma flowers again.

Mom told me this heartbreaking story after I'd reached adulthood. So, it had no effect on the way I felt about my grandparents while I was young.

From my child's perspective, Grandma and Grandpa were the ones you would pick if you had ten thousand pairs of grandparents to choose from. And selecting a greeting card for either one of them was as easy as being their grandchild. (Grandma's probable extreme politics notwithstanding.)

The satisfaction of choosing a card for one of my grandparents, however, only amplified the heartache involved in finding the right cards for Mom and Dad.

Especially Dad. Only the most generalized and impersonal card would do for him. The effusive cards expressing heartfelt sentiments never applied. Even the light-hearted funny ones seldom conveyed a sentiment remotely relevant. In fact, they all came across as disingenuous and, frankly, just wrong.

Most "dad cards" enumerated all of a father's best attributes – his steadfast role as the pillar of the family, his emotional strength, his counsel, his wisdom, his endless support, his being the one his child could count on when no one else seemed to be on her side.

I adored my dad, but not one of these qualities described him.

Honestly, Dad wasn't even the head of our family, much less its pillar. His emotional "distance" limited all of his relationships. His atypical brand of guidance had its occasional merit, but not as described in any greeting card I've ever seen.

I grew up dreading Father's Day and Dad's birthday, all because of the cloud of depression that hung over every trip to the store to find the right card for Dad.

So, with Father's Day or Dad's birthday fast approaching, I would buck up, don all the emotional armor I could muster, and go to the drug store. All the while I'd pray the right card would be among the first few I'd see so my agony would be short-lived.

Let me be clear about the unpleasantness of these shopping excursions. It wasn't just about the difficulty of finding an appropriate card when almost none seemed to fit. It had far more to do with the disappointing periodic reminder that none of those admirable fatherly traits described my dad.

Finding the right cards for Mom wasn't much easier. But the situation with Mom was more complex. She certainly made my early life exceedingly difficult by robbing me of a large part of my own identity. But lest you believe she was all doom and gloom, I will offer some countervailing details. Maybe a story or two would help to illustrate what I mean.

In her later years Mom came to be known to many relatives and family friends as "the martini lady." No, she wasn't a lush. But she would have a martini every afternoon, as regular as clockwork. A day of Mom's wasn't complete unless she'd enjoyed a dry gin martini at precisely 4:00 p.m.

Mom also possessed an impressive collection of martini glasses. I think it numbered close to a hundred specimens, each one unique. When one of us found an unusual new glass to add to the assortment, it made a great gift for Mom on her birthday or Mother's Day.

Mom was such a fan of martinis, she carried a small atomizer filled with vermouth in her purse. That way, when dining out she could add her own vermouth to straight gin to ensure her martini was "dry as a bone."

I'll never forget the time I drew a line in the sand, believing Mom had taken the vermouth atomizer routine too far. That evening there was a sizable group of us at a restaurant. Mom *strongly* recommended that anyone intending to have a martini should order it with no vermouth, and we'd simply pass around her atomizer.

As I recall, everyone complied, except me. I thought there was something a little unseemly about Mom's "suggestion." It felt too controlling, as things with Mom often did. I wanted my drink prepared by the bartender without my having to alter it. I'd order it dry and take my chances while trusting the barman to heed my wishes.

At some point, a very nice "martini tradition" started. Mom had issued an open invitation for family friends to join her at her home for a drink. So, when one of my pals or Bob's happened to be near Mom's house in the late afternoon, they knew they were welcome to stop in to have a martini with Mom. They would simply call and let her know they were on their way.

Please understand, what I am describing are young people in their 30's or 40's enthusiastically dropping in on my mother for a martini. Mom was in her 70's and 80's when these visits were frequent events.

The truth is, Mom possessed outstanding social skills and a terrific sense of humor. Even to our friends who were thirty or forty years her junior, she was lots of fun.

One more memory brings a smile to my face...

When I was thirteen, Mom was up in arms over my use of our family's telephone. It's not as if she could tell me to end my call to go finish my homework. When you read Chapter 6, you will find out why Mom knew, without having to ask, that my homework was already done.

You can imagine the scenario: My homework complete and household chores finished (I'd even made my daily call to Grandma and Grandpa), I wanted to phone my friends. And when I called a friend, it was a two-hour conversation, give or take. Hey, I was a teenager!

Mom complained nightly about not having a phone available to call *her* friends.

My fourteenth birthday happened to be a school day. I arrived home and headed straight to my bedroom to drop off my textbooks and other school stuff. Since the minutest details of my bedroom remained precisely the same each and every day (you'll also read about my neatness compulsion in Chapter 6), I would immediately notice anything newly added.

Well, that day I observed something new all right, a wonderful addition that hadn't been there when I'd left for school that morning. On my desk was a brand-new telephone, and it wasn't an extension. *It had its own number.* I now had my very own phone, in my bedroom, with its own phone number!

I was so excited I jumped up and down while squealing.

Mom and Dad, of course, were pleased I was so surprised and thrilled.

Mom quipped, "This is your birthday present but, honestly, it's more for me than for you. We're glad you're happy, Sweetie."

In any case, perhaps you can simply take my word for it that selecting a greeting card for Dad was the worst shopping experience imaginable. And choosing one for Mom was a lesser but comparable nightmare.

When I married my husband Sam, whose near perfection as a husband rivaled that of Grandma and Grandpa as grandparents, I once again had someone in my life for whom shopping for cards would be a happy experience. There may have been thirty anniversary cards on the rack, and all of them were a perfect choice for my Sam. All I had to do was joyfully examine them while searching for the most special one of all.

Have I inadvertently identified a direct correlation between the ease of finding just the right greeting card and the recipient's ability to maintain healthy human bonds?

Perhaps one could apply this hypothesis as a litmus test for entering into close relationships: If you are pleased to shop for a greeting card for the person, he/she is probably a worthy candidate to be your friend or spouse.

Chapter Four
How Feminism Failed to Deliver

A real man treats his woman the same way he would expect another man to treat his daughter. – Anonymous

When feminism began in the early 1970s, I was all in. The movement promised to improve everything in women's lives –

work, romance, family life. You name it. Who wouldn't want things to be even better?

In retrospect, the reality for me was pretty sobering. Of course, there were some favorable outcomes. But on balance, I believe the impact of feminism on my life was a substantial net negative.

I seek solely to relate my experience at the forefront of this immense cultural shift. Like so many others of the era, I was essentially an unwitting guinea pig for an untested crusade whose objectives may have changed some of our society's conventions and values too radically.

I only know how the societal transformation impacted me at the time. I can't help viewing it as a "speed bump" of enormous consequence.

Growing up, I could never quite figure out why I possessed so little self-confidence. All I knew was, God had unluckily "endowed" me with the most unflattering hair imaginable, high myopia (extreme near-sightedness) and a flat chest – not exactly the makings of a Homecoming queen.

Presumably with the best of intentions, my personality-plus mother had sought to mold me into a replica of herself. Or perhaps she'd had a perverse need for self-validation. In any case, every opinion I expressed, no matter the subject, had to be identical to hers. My own impressions were thoroughly suppressed.

A lack of freedom to develop my own tastes and judgments appeared to hinder the evolution of my social skills, as well.

I seemed to have no individualism, character or sense of humor I could call my own. In social situations, I found myself attempting in vain to copy the wit and conversational styles of others just to get by. I failed miserably.

It took me years to realize Mom had presented me with a truly impossible dilemma: Mirroring another person's thoughts, tastes and judgments was a feat only a bona fide mind reader could successfully pull off.

I recall the day Mom took me shopping for party shoes. I was four years old. We walked up to the shoe store's window, which displayed a wide selection of girls' dressy shoes.

Mom asked me which ones I liked, and without hesitation I pointed to a pair of pink patent leather Mary-Janes.

Mom harshly snapped, "We're getting black ones!"

As she scolded me, Mom angrily yanked on my arm, pulling her stumbling child through the door and into the shop.

I wondered what in the world I'd done to upset Mom.

Moreover, I'm pretty sure I never again dared to express another opinion of my own, at least not for a good thirty years. Instead, when called upon to make a judgment, or express matters of taste, I did my best to guess what Mom's response would be.

Mom had always maintained a highly judgmental character, however arbitrary and ultimately changeable her views later proved to be. Even so, her friends and relatives were expected to agree with her every idea, taste and whim. If not, they would suffer my mother's displeasure, whether spoken or unspoken.

Mom's expectations for compliance fell especially hard on my shoulders.

As we've established, I embraced Mom's opinions and tastes, thoroughly squelching my own. There simply seemed to be no other choice. But at age eight, eleven, twenty, even thirty-five, when her views didn't always seem to agree with my experience, I assumed my experience, or my interpretation of that experience, was somehow erroneous.

It never occurred to me Mom might be wrong.

In any case, my mother, who had a certification in early childhood development, parented with everything she had to give. She claimed to love me beyond words, although I doubted the fact for much of my early adulthood. The parents whose children were enrolled in Mom's co-op nursery school certainly thought the world of her and frequently reminded me how lucky I was to be her daughter.

Perhaps Mom's child rearing methods might have been a blessing for another girl – for example, one with an inherently spirited disposition. (On second thought, she and Mom might well have started a nuclear war.)

But a mother more encouraging of her daughter's natural self might have proven a better match for me. Of course, I'll never know for sure.

And in spite of all this, I suppose it's possible some inborn failing within myself, and not Mom's overbearing will, could be responsible for the exceptionally late harvest of what became my rather formidable identity. But it seems unlikely, especially given a blessed and much-needed tidbit of validation offered to me in my early 20s.

I received a phone call from Mom's best friend Katy, whom I'd always adored. Katy had been my nursery school teacher, and she was kind, loving and lots of fun.

"Vicki dear, I want to talk to you about something. Can you come over to my house one day this week after you finish work?" Katy requested.

I'm pretty sure Katy had never called me before, even though I'd known her my entire life. We saw each other at gatherings of various kinds, she'd come to our house, or we'd go to hers. I was intensely curious as to what could be on her mind to bring about such an unusual invitation.

"I can come over at about 5:00 on Wednesday?" I suggested in response to Katy.

"Fine, honey. See you then."

I was filled with anticipation until Wednesday finally arrived. I couldn't wait to find out what Katy intended for our talk.

At about the halfway point as I climbed the steep steps to Katy's front door, I noticed she was waiting for me at the top. She seemed anxious to begin our conversation.

I went inside, and Katy offered me tea and cookies.

She proposed, "Let's go sit in the living room."

Once we were seated, Katy looked at me with an intense gaze.

Slowly enunciating for maximal dramatic impact, she asked, "What's it like being the daughter of God?"

I immediately knew Katy had made no religious reference. She was referring, of course, to her sometimes authoritarian and always-had-to-be-right closest friend... my mother.

Initially, I didn't know how to answer Katy's question, and was pretty sure it was rhetorical, anyway. But I was beyond grateful she'd asked it. I finally had verification, some understanding and sympathy from someone who knew Mom well, for what I'd experienced growing up.

Regaining my composure after Katy's monumental revelation, I wondered what exactly had prompted this turn of events.

I confirmed that being my mother's daughter had been anything but easy. But my recollection of the rest of the interchange is hazy. I don't remember if Katy gave me many details of what appeared to be a rift between her and Mom. I only know it would be one of several before they eventually distanced themselves permanently from one another.

So, with Mom's contribution to my early life issues left to my gentle readers' judgment, let's talk about Dad. In the face of Mom's reign as mother, father, head-of-household, "chief cook and bottle washer," Dad seemed, and probably felt, a bit extraneous. At any rate, the role seemed to suit him.

Well, that didn't suit me. I wanted a dad like Jim Anderson, the crème de la crème of paternal perfection played by

Robert Young in the 1950's sit-com *Father Knows Best* – a dad who would make me so sure of what I should expect from boys, and later men, there was no chance I would ever sell myself short.

Jim Anderson made his daughters feel like princesses. He protected them. And above all, he presented them with a model of a good man – a marriageable man – so well defined, only the most extreme daughterly stupidity might have resulted in a poor choice of a husband.

Okay, maybe I overstate the case. I'm only suggesting I would love to have been cherished… just a little.

My father was no Jim Anderson, not even close.

But Dad could be pretty cool. He was tall, handsome, intelligent, and athletic. When he took a running dive into my aunt and uncle's swimming pool, everyone took notice of his power, finesse and flawless form. And as we know, he turned me into an ace with a baseball glove.

Dad loved to trespass onto fenced residential construction sites. I enthusiastically accompanied him on these "dangerous" missions, delighting in the fantasy I might one day own such a home. I enjoyed guessing which room of the barely wood-framed structure I was standing in. Climbing around on staircases with no railings, and on second-story platforms with missing walls, seemed so daring. Not to mention the rusty nails strewn about, any one of which, if stepped on, might have rendered me hopelessly afflicted with lock-jaw!

In fact, exploring construction sites was the least treacherous of the instances during my childhood in which Dad put me in grave danger. It's like the old adage, "A cat has nine lives." You could say I was the kid with three or four lives. Allow me to elaborate…

When I was three, and Bobby just one, our family ventured out for a day at the beach. Mom laid a big blanket on the sand, on which we could all hang out. There was even room for the picnic basket.

Dad had gone to the restroom near the parking lot behind us. Mom, Bob and I sat atop the blanket facing the ocean. Dad returned from the restroom running toward the water, clearly intending to make a dramatic entry.

On his way past our blanket, Dad reached down with one arm and scooped me up. Barely slowing down to "collect" me, and with me haphazardly tucked under one arm, he continued his sprint into the ocean.

I vaguely recall having a minute or two of fun as Dad swam further and further out while taking care to keep my head above water. What happened next was truly shocking.

A huge wave appeared, looming over us and threatening to drown every swimmer in the immediate area. Dad panicked.

The next thing I remember is rolling up on the beach coughing and sputtering. I could see Dad frantically looking all over for me, while Mom was jumping up and down on the blanket pointing to the current location of her half-drowned elder child.

Dad followed the direction of Mom's finger to the spot where I'd washed up on the wet sand. He hurried over to recover his three-year-old, and took me back to the blanket. Honestly, I thought Mom would kill Dad. But he lived to commit the next offense, which happened a few years later.

Dad loved taking weekend drives on old mountain roads outside L.A. Sometimes the whole family would go. But more often than not, Dad had to talk one of us into accompanying him on his Sunday jaunt.

On this occasion, I'd decided to venture out with Dad into the local mountains. I was about nine.

I mentioned Dad loved to ignore "NO TRESPASSING" signs.

Well, we will extend the definition to include the posted notices on curvy mountain roads that read, "DO NOT GO BEYOND THIS POINT."

It had been a lovely drive with beautiful scenery, a true getaway from the "concrete jungle" of the big city. We'd even stopped at a favorite diner for oyster stew, a dish Dad and I both favored, and which set us apart from the rest of the family.

After a while Dad came upon a barricade fully blocking the road ahead and displaying one of *those notices.*

What did my pop do? Dad being Dad, he decided to ignore the posted warning!

A little nervous at this decision, I remained vigilant… just in case.

A moment later I let out a horrified scream.

"Sto-o-o-o-op!!!"

Dad calmly applied the brakes to stop the car, casually asking, "What? What? What's a matter?"

"Get out and *look*!" I cried in disbelief.

We both opened our doors and carefully exited the car. The front tires of Dad's '65 Camaro were no more than six inches from a sheer drop-off, where a section of road had washed out and fallen down the mountain.

I don't believe Mom ever found out about this little incident. If she had, I really think she would have wasted no time filing for divorce.

About a year later, we took a three-week family vacation, a driving trip, to see some of the national parks. While touring through Yellowstone, Dad stopped the car by the side of the road where we'd spotted a moose standing a short distance away.

We were all so excited to see the animal up close.

Dad instructed me, "Vicki, grab the camera and get a picture!"

I rolled down my window and pointed the camera toward the moose.

Dad demanded, "No, get out and get up close to it."

At which point Mom quietly, but loudly enough for me to hear, asked Dad, "Do you think that's a good idea?"

"Sure, it's fine," Dad answered.

I nervously exited the car and proceeded to photograph the moose.

Before I had a chance to snap a picture, Dad called out, "Get closer!"

Positioning myself far too close to the moose, I quickly took the photo and ran back to the car.

In retrospect, what Dad forced me to do that day was foolish, and needlessly risky.

The truth is, I both idolized Dad and thought he was pretty nutty. At the very least, we can all agree he was more than capable of exhibiting poor judgment.

Furthermore, it became apparent early on, Mom had assumed most of his role in our household, as well as her own. And Dad had allowed it. So, we were a somewhat dysfunctional example of the typical American family.

Even so, I might have made it through childhood and young adulthood relatively unscathed, emotionally speaking, except for one thing. The women's movement happened. And Mom was all about this flowering victory of secular progressivism. What was worse, she was determined to live it vicariously through me.

I was a teenager when the women's movement first took on steam. Much of the hype was frivolous stuff like bra burning. On the more productive side, it forced strict changes, some of them helpful, to women's treatment in the office environment and throughout society.

By the time I started my first job as a mechanical engineer, I was right there on the front lines witnessing the birth of corporate sexual harassment policy. I also observed various instances of managerial "hand-slapping" of mischievous male employees who would test the limits of the "oppressive" new rules. It sure was an interesting time, if also a confusing one.

I guess I have the women's movement to thank for much of the ready acceptance I received in the workplace, for women engineers were a rare commodity in the 1970's.

I also credit the movement for rendering the roles of men and women in romantic relationships hopelessly ambiguous.

Let's back up a bit to September of 1972, when I would begin my stint at university. My parents drove me and my worldly belongings from our home in Los Angeles to San Diego, about one hundred miles south. I would be moving into the dormitory room I would occupy as a freshman at UC San Diego. I was excited and scared.

Why go away to college? I must have sensed on some level a vital need to put some distance between me and Mom. Doing so might provide a chance for my identity, assuming I had one, to finally emerge.

Little did I know, it would be many years before my rather playful and self-assured persona would come out of hiding. But at the time, I was hopeful my personality's debut was lurking right around the corner.

In truth, I was more than hopeful. I was *desperate*.

Mom, Dad, and I arrived at the campus on a Saturday afternoon. School would start on Monday. My roommate, Joleen, had obviously moved in, but she wasn't around. None of the other girls in the five-room suite were anywhere to be found, either.

Mom and Dad kissed me good-bye and left me to unpack into the half of the room remaining empty. The folks would not be staying the night, but would immediately be on their way home. I recall feeling strangely relieved when they left. I felt ready for this.

As the afternoon wore on, some of my suite mates returned. They seemed nice enough and invited me to have dinner with them in La Jolla, as one of them had a car. The dinner outing sounded like fun, and I had a little spending money. So, a small group of us departed for our first off-campus excursion as residents of our very affluent new town.

When we returned from dinner, I had no idea as to the shock awaiting me. I entered my dorm room to find Joleen, the roommate I had yet to meet, in *my* bed with some guy. I ran out of the room pretty much traumatized and making a sizable fuss. I think I even burst into tears. Two of the girls I'd just dined with took me aside to authoritatively explain all about the "facts of college life." I listened astutely.

Oh, of course I already knew about sex. I just hadn't experienced it myself. Nor had any of the friends I'd hung out with in high school. We had been the scholastically gifted kids, a bit on the nerdy side, and light petting was about as far as any of us had ever gone. I guess I had expected the dormitory at UCSD to be pretty much a level playing field with respect to sex. Boy, was I ever wrong.

Joleen had hailed from a Southern California beach town. She was a surfer. I quickly learned a thing or two about surfer girls. They apparently knew all about sex from first-hand experience. According to the stereotype, it seemed they had quite the reputation.

I wondered... what about the university's purported screening of roommates for compatibility? I guessed the criteria were less than comprehensive.

Accepting my new reality, I soon calmed down. Joleen and I were cordial, but never became close. I began dating a nice, fairly conservative guy named Ron. I also began to feel great pressure to lose my virginity. And having been raised with no real guidelines for preserving my self-respect, frankly I couldn't think of reasons to say no.

As pathetic as it sounds, I couldn't justify saying no to sex.

Everything around me was screaming, "Why not?" "What's the harm?" "It's cool." "Everybody's doing it." "It's the sexual revolution, you know."

Not ready for sex, I found myself in a minefield of sexual expectation.

There were additional, rather surprising, elements adding to the pressure to have sex. Some weekends I would go home to see my parents and high school friends. Mom would excitedly ask me for the details of my life at the university. I would tell her everything worthy of mention.

And in a last-ditch effort to find a way to save my self-worth, I told Mom some of the sexual particulars of life in the UCSD dorms. Maybe she would finally enlighten me with a reason to say no to sex. I was truly hoping for her sage wisdom and guidance.

Guidance is exactly what I got, but it wasn't of the variety I desperately wanted and needed. And it certainly wasn't wise.

When the subject of sex came up, Mom's eyes opened wide with intense interest. She told me how lucky I was to be reaching adulthood at a time when sexual taboos were on their way out. Mom gratefully praised the women's movement for this "fabulous" cultural development.

Great. Just great.

For the next year or so, I just went through the motions of university life, still trying to just copy others, for I had no clue how to act, socialize, or just be myself. My boyfriend Ron was the picture of patience and decency, and he never pressured me sexually.

Then something unexpected happened. The teaching assistant for my Physics class invited me over. Phil was a graduate student working on his PhD. I'd had a little crush on him and was quite flattered by the invitation. I went to his apartment, innocently thinking he wanted to get to know me better as a friend.

It turned out, of course, Phil assumed sex was a given. More confused than ever, I felt backed into a corner. In spite of my loyalty to Ron, and believing I needed to submit to sex with Phil to correct *my mistake,* I lost my virginity that night to a man I barely knew, and who'd had no idea it was my first time.

Why hadn't Dad been more like Jim Anderson? Why couldn't Mom have given me something other than mixed signals and erroneous messages during my journey to adulthood? Why in the world hadn't either or both of them ever given me just one reason to say *no*?!

But they never did.

Okay, so Mom was confused, too. She knew nothing but contempt for conservative values. Progressivism was what she subscribed to, and her intentions were all good. After all, she wasn't the only one buying into the new "sexual freedom."

How can I blame her, or Dad for that matter, for the intolerable and bewildering circumstances in which I found myself? My parents were as much generationally removed products of the new era of sexual promiscuity as I was a product of their marriage.

The prior year, I remember being asked out by a boy I liked in high school. He called to invite me to a movie. In my innocence and excitement, my inclination was to enthusiastically accept. But Mom whispered to me her recommendation that I should tell him I wasn't sure if I could go. I should play hard to get.

I did what Mom suggested, even though I felt ridiculous. And I could tell the boy knew exactly what was going on. Mom finally issued the A-OK for me to accept the invitation.

When the boy arrived to pick me up, Mom insisted on answering the door while I stayed in the back of the house.

She then called out, "Vicki, your gentleman caller is here."

Why the sudden conservatism? Why the turn-of-the-century vernacular? My first impulse was to be embarrassed. But as always, I assumed Mom knew what she was doing.

In any case, where my date with this boy could have been a joyous experience, instead I was so confused I barely said a word all evening.

So here I was in college, having been encouraged in the past to play hard to get and to behave like some sort of nouveau debutante when my dates came to call for me. Now I guessed I was supposed to have sex with anyone who bought me a coke.

I felt like a Victorian-era fallen princess whose natural modesty and directness were systematically being contested by constantly changing cultural mores about which I knew nothing.

I began to gain weight. I also became terribly depressed – the only prolonged depression of my life. That unrelenting sadness would, unfortunately, see me through the remainder of my college years.

During my second year at UCSD, I was so miserable I would return from class and go to bed. That's right, having arisen at 7 a.m., I was going back to sleep at around lunch time. It was the only way I knew to escape some of the pain of my overweight, identity-less life.

My roommate Valerie and other girls at school were having a wonderful time. I was at a complete loss to understand why this was happening to me.

I had been a fantastic student all through high school. A wonderful group of friends had provided a cherished emotional "second home." I had participated in loads of extracurricular activities, including having been the concert mistress of our school orchestra and a baton twirler with the band.

What had gone so wrong? Why was I struggling to get myself to study? Why had I become overweight for the only time in my life? Why was I so persistently and profoundly depressed?

I was "encouraged" by one thing and one thing only – I was scared to death I would attempt suicide. I rightly figured my fear would keep me from doing so, leaving open the possibility things might get better sometime in the future. This was my first glimpse of the steadfast survivor residing within me.

I began a third year at UCSD but couldn't take more of the same. After two weeks, I called my folks. Crying over the phone, I begged my parents to let me come home.

They were, thankfully, more than happy to have me return to the nest. Dad said he'd be there the very next day to bring me and my worldly belongings home.

I took the quarter off from school, getting a job at a local family-run eatery near our house. My childhood friend Aaron sweetly told me I wasn't fat, but just voluptuous. I guessed things might start to get better. I'd applied for a transfer to UCLA's engineering school and would start there the following quarter.

Engineering school was a struggle. The course material was challenging, but not a problem for me given I'd always had a natural aptitude for math. But I was unsuccessfully battling my weight, and still so depressed. My self-image had never been lower, which is saying quite a lot when looking back on the way I'd felt about my appearance all through elementary school and junior high.

At least I'd had a reprieve in high school, a time during which I'd been considered fairly attractive. But hadn't I suffered enough?

Apparently not. Since I would be hopeless and sad during what was supposed to be the best time of my life, perhaps I would learn something that would serve me well later on.

"Spoken" like a true survivor.

I spent the two years of engineering school in a perpetually unhappy state of mind. I made friends and participated in the student chapter of the Society of Women Engineers. But I couldn't shake the feeling I was worthless.

Furthermore, a curious notion began to dawn on me… Maybe I had chosen an engineering major for a reason other than my ease with mathematics and a desire for an engineering career.

With a slowly blooming clarity, I had to admit becoming an engineer would make me the perfect example of the "success" of the women's movement. *Mom would approve.* Perhaps of even greater significance, I felt more comfortable in an environment in which I wasn't competing with other women.

It made so much sense. At UCLA engineering school, I would sometimes be the lone female in a class of sixty students. It gave me a way to feel a tiny bit special. I was unique and noticeable. That was something, at least.

There was another, wholly practical, reason for choosing engineering. It was one of the few majors with which a graduate could snag a great job with only a bachelor's degree.

Priority number one was to get myself out of my parents' house, financially independent of them, *and away from Mom.* Engineering was my ticket to getting there as quickly as possible.

I've sometimes wondered... what might my major have been if not for these circumstances of necessity?

Believe it or not, I've always fantasized about singing and dancing on the musical theater stage.

Would I have made it on Broadway?

There is simply no way to know what path my childhood and adolescence might have taken had I not spent those years striving to be a carbon copy of my mother.

After engineering school, I got my first job as a mechanical engineer at a manufacturing plant – an aluminum works. The pay was decent and, being one of only two women engineers there, I still felt special. I rented my own apartment about thirty miles away from my parents' house – again, putting a little distance between me and Mom. The independence was exactly what I needed.

Although I still had a long road to traverse to my ultimate goal of social maturity and emotional autonomy, I finally had some breathing room.

Then a funny thing happened. The weight dropped off! Just as I had resigned myself to living the rest of my life twenty to thirty pounds overweight, and having tried many diets to no avail, the extra weight just came off. The 155 pounds became a perfect 125, which was just right for my 5'5" medium frame.

With a new lease on life and my appearance, I was getting more dates. I seldom spent an evening at home. If I didn't have a date, I met a friend for dinner or a symphony concert. I was living what seemed like the perfect single person's life. And it wasn't half bad.

Thanks to the women's movement, I now knew exactly what to expect from men. They were to treat me as their equal, just like one of the guys. It was now considered an insult to the woman if a man opened the door for her. And pretty, feminine clothing was a no-no, as was make-up of any kind.

There were only two problems. First of all, I didn't particularly like posing as an *equivalent* to men, wherein all differences between us were to go unnoticed. On the job, some aspects of it were clearly beneficial. But socially, it left me feeling empty and disappointed.

Second, I found I still had no faith whatsoever in my own tastes and opinions. I couldn't even buy a pair of shoes or a t-shirt without seeking Mom's approval. If she didn't like the item, I returned it to the store.

Conversely, if Mom bought me a dress I didn't care for, I said I loved it, assuming she was right and I was wrong. I'd dutifully wear the garment, berating myself for the fact it wouldn't have been my choice. My closet was a testament to my mother's good taste, my apartment's furniture and décor examples of the same.

I began to realize my dependence upon Mom was thoroughly unhealthy at this point. I embarked on a campaign to learn to trust my own judgment. The first step in this process, however, was a toughy. I determined it would be necessary to convince myself of my mother's fallibility – in essence, her ability to *be wrong.*

How hard would that be?

Unbelievably, this first step took me another fifteen years to complete. At age 40, I would at long last be free. Once I became satisfied of the arbitrary and utterly flawed nature of my mother's judgments, I really was able to toss them aside. Mine took over and I never looked back.

The test, it turned out, was a dress I'd bought in my early 40's. Mom said it looked "skimpy" on me, but I liked it. Would I still feel attractive wearing it? Thank goodness, I would and did.

In the meantime, though, I was still struggling through my 20s and 30s. I was as confused as ever.

There was a conservative young woman I befriended who didn't put much stock in the women's movement. She was a Southern belle who'd recently moved to California from Atlanta. I outwardly expressed my disapproval of her somewhat negative attitude toward feminism. Deep down I was envious. She wore make-up and nice clothes. She dated men who treated her well. She valued her femininity and exuded self-confidence.

My long-time chum Aaron and I would go out as friends, which was an enormous blessing in disguise. Aaron, who was very conservative at the time, didn't buy into feminism, either.

We would go to nice restaurants, concerts, and plays. Aaron insisted I dress up for these occasions. I made fun of him, but obliged, more willingly than I would admit at the time. I secretly liked being treated as a woman, even by a man who was nothing more than a friend.

The truth is, Aaron offered me some lessons I believe my parents should have taught me. Unfortunately, the women's movement was a powerful overlord, rendering my parents incapable of understanding its destructive aspects. Hence, I proved a very slow learner in response to Aaron's coaching.

I would spend the next few years floundering around in my career, and choosing the wrong men to date, while enjoying my friends and a variety of cultural activities. Then I would marry the wrong man, and stay married to him for five years before finally divorcing. Thank goodness we hadn't had children.

As a result of my divorce, I felt enormous relief. I also felt I had committed the ultimate failure. But the feeling was relatively short-lived, for I soon realized I had serendipitously happened upon long overdue clarity in regard to one important thing – I now knew exactly what I wanted in a husband.

Part II
Obsessed

Chapter Five
Missed Opportunities and a Pickle Vendor

Life's missed opportunities, in the end, may seem more poignant to us than those we embraced – because in our imagination they have a perfection that reality can never rival. – Roger Ebert

As a teenager and young adult, there were many instances in which I rejected a nice young man in favor of a "bad boy." I knew I was making a mistake, but I didn't care. You could call it an obsession. And obsessions tend to attribute to the type A.

"Bad boys" amount to "speed bumps" for the young women who adore them, for these unfortunate idols of their girlfriends' admiration are emotionally limited young men incapable of maintaining fulfilling relationships. Hence, this obsession will always result in heartache.

What is it about young women and the ne'er-do-wells to whom they become attracted?

What is so desirable about a bad boy, anyway? In my case, it wasn't so much my swooning over bad boys in general. Specifically, I would fall for a certain sub-category of the "bad boy" – *the dark brooding type*. (Think: Marlon Brando, James Dean, Val Kilmer and Jane Eyre's Mr. Rochester.) Either way, we're talking about a guy who will very likely meter out crumbs of affection while maintaining his emotional distance from she who worships him. It can't possibly end well.

Yes, in my younger days I went for the gloomy "lord of darkness," otherwise known as the "mystery man."

A few years ago, I met a nice-looking, outgoing and personable young man in his 20s who complained about the women his age. They didn't seem to dig him. They liked him as a friend, but fell for the guys who broke their hearts.

He told me, he tried being there at just the right moment to pick up the pieces and do damage control. He reasonably expected the girl to have finally had enough of the bad boys. She will have learned her lesson, he thought. He would then swoop in to offer himself up as a princely alternative after the girl had come to her senses.

Seems logical, right? But to his amazement, these women went right back for more, choosing over and over again to entrust their hearts to emotionally limited and unavailable men.

I smiled knowingly, able to thoroughly identify with this phenomenon from my own personal experience. I told the young man to relax and enjoy himself, because everything would change when he was about thirty-five.

So, it seems mostly true that nice guys finish last, but only until the women in their age group "grow up."

Popular thought suggests women mature early. So, why are the good men waiting into their thirties for the women to get with the program?

I believe women's purported early maturity is generally limited to their physical attributes. Emotionally, many women don't get it together for decades. And some never do.

You know the type – the 45-year-old woman with a string of disastrous relationships behind her. She constantly bashes men, declaring there are no good ones out there, only swine.

I am so grateful not to be one of those women. It took me way too long to grow up, but at least it happened.

For me, the transformation to preferring nice men occurred in a relatively abrupt revelation. There must have been a trigger, but apparently it wasn't memorable enough to stay with me.

All I know is, I suddenly saw the dark brooding types as the dregs of society, hapless loners in need of psychotherapy. They were cowards to be pitied, not brave warriors to be coveted. I began to see the well-adjusted, well parented, happy man as the strong and attractive one.

About this same time, I happened to see a particular movie. All told, the sequence of events would bode well for my future.

But first, let's take a little voyage into the world of squandered opportunities...

In high school, my "lord of darkness" was Ted, the first chair trumpet player in the school orchestra. And yes, he was pretty darn shy and brooding. I thought he was gorgeous.

Ted was one of very few of my circle of high school friends to possess his own car. With Ted's "wheels" available to us, our little group of intellectual crowd pals could easily get to wherever it is geeky teenagers hang out in their well-behaved nerdiness. On one occasion we managed to squeeze ten of us into Ted's little sedan. I guess we weren't going very far.

I recall we had summer parties at the homes of friends who had backyard swimming pools. There were also a few progressive dinners, and some trips to the beach.

I hated those beach trips. After only twenty minutes of laying out in the sun, I would be frightfully sunburned and exceedingly bored. But I digress...

One of the boys in our group was an old soul we'll call Ben. He wasn't great looking nor particularly well dressed. But there was something so comfortable and centered about him. And he had a subtle charisma that charmed everyone who knew him. All of the girls in our little clique were crazy about him. And Ben was crazy about me.

Ben and I would talk on the phone for hours every evening, discussing very deep subjects of a philosophical nature. We would write poetry and short stories to share with each other. We were wonderful friends.

So, there I was, in the enviable position of being able to choose between Ted and Ben. In spite of Ben being the very example of a happy, stable, sensitive and self-assured young man, it would be years before I would find someone like him irresistible. Even so, I was quite attracted to him. But my teenage fantasies were too strong an influence. I chose my lord of darkness – my trumpeter – Ted.

There really isn't much more to say. I dated Ted for the next year or two. And Ben dated one of the other girls in our clique. The eight or ten of us continued to socialize as a group, for the most part.

I, of course, thought I was in love with Ted. And Ted was a very nice guy. But he wasn't Ben. Ben was special, and I was well aware of the fact. Still, I willfully declined the chance to be his girlfriend.

A few years later, I was finishing my engineering degree at UCLA. As I mentioned earlier, my college years had been the most painful of my life. Remember, thanks to my mother's expectation that I reach adulthood as her exact replica, I had no discernible identity of my own. This situation had been problematic throughout my childhood, but became completely untenable as I navigated college and young adulthood.

Having ballooned up to 155 pounds, I was green with envy at the sight of my pretty *and thin* female classmates.

Apart from attending classes, I took a side job on campus as manager of the Engineering Society "food lounge" (sort of a glorified snack bar). My duties were to staff and supervise the employees of the popular hangout.

One of my team was a very attractive, hard-working young man named Mark. He restocked the shelves, cleaned the tables and swept the floor. He kept the place immaculate. I began to develop a crush on him the moment we met.

After a few months of occasional chats with Mark, I worked up the courage to ask him if I could treat him to lunch the following week. To my surprise, he seemed thrilled and enthusiastically accepted my invitation. We agreed to have lunch the following Thursday.

Thursday arrived, and Mark showed up in a dress shirt for our lunch date! I should have been elated over the knowledge Mark seemed just as interested in me as I was in him.

But alas, I was too emotionally confused at the time to take advantage of this unexpected blessing. The truth is, I felt wholly unworthy of Mark's attention. I didn't feel at all attractive, or womanly, and consequently found myself unable to behave like a date instead of a boss. Lunch was a dud, and it was entirely my fault.

Mark had been a willing and attentive gentleman. And I couldn't handle it.

Some years later, in my late twenties, I met a nice man named Steve at a party. He asked me out, suggesting we find a movie we might enjoy. My brother Bob had been prodding me to see *American Werewolf in London*. I told Steve that Bob generally had pretty good taste in movies, so maybe we should give it a try. He was in complete agreement.

Steve and I both found the movie lacking in substance, and chuckled at Bob's now highly questionable movie recommendation karma. The two of us really seemed to hit it off.

The following week, Steve called and told me he would love to come over and cook me dinner – his "world famous" Chicken Nottingham. I saw no reason to turn Steve down. His only request of me was a suitably set table. Other than that, I got pampered to the max with a delicious three-course meal, including dessert. He even insisted on washing the dishes.

Once again, Steve and I got along beautifully, passing another evening with an easy, comfortable rapport. He got my sense of humor, and I got his.

Sounds pretty perfect, doesn't it? At the very least, I might have acknowledged strong potential for Steve and me.

Yeah, try convincing she who still dreamt each night of her varied and sundry dark brooding men of mystery. The draw was still too strong. There was a dark brooding type at work whom I'd had my eye on. We'd even dated a couple of times, and he was still expressing interest in seeing more of me. Frankly, the very promising Steve proved a mere distraction.

The following weekend, Steve surprised me by attending the annual concert gala of the orchestra in which I played violin. He even brought flowers. I all but ignored him. I couldn't help myself. At the time, it was all about the gravitational pull of the bad boy at work who was destined to break my heart.

Looking back on these bright chances foregone, I could "flog" myself with condemnations of "stupid, stupid, *stupid!*"

But for many of us the road from childhood to adulthood is agonizing, and we learn many lessons the hard way. So, I could beat myself up, but why? What's done is done.

Thank you, kind reader, for staying with me to this point. It was painful for me, too. But you are about to be rewarded, and handsomely.

This is the story of the pickle vendor, and how I met my second husband Sam, the man who could have taught seminars on how to be the world's most wonderful husband.

Not long after divorcing my first husband, I saw a movie and was particularly impressed by the male lead character whose name happened to be *Sam*. Sam was a good, kind, hard-working

Jewish man with moral fiber and inner strength. He sold pickles on the lower East side of Manhattan. He was in no way a brooding lord of darkness and, hence, he was the kind of man who would never have interested me in the least. But that was before.

Soon after seeing the movie, I called my childhood friend Mindy.

"Mindela, I just saw *Crossing Delancey!*

Mindy enthusiastically replied, "Oh, wasn't that good?"

"Yes!" I answered. "But what's more important is, now I know what kind of man I should be with... a nice Jewish man from New York named Sam."

Take note of my phrasing here. The first word in my description is "nice," that over-used, unimaginative word used by people when there is nothing very extraordinary in the thing they are describing. It is merely *nice*.

For me, on the other hand, the use of the word "nice" to describe a man I might like to meet was wholly symbolic of my blossoming emotional health and maturity. In this sense, "nice" signaled a breakthrough of a pretty gargantuan magnitude.

But why should the man be Jewish? I am Jewish, though raised in a very secular home. Even without the religious aspect, there are things that Jews have in common. There is a humor and a sensibility, a tradition. The food alone speaks volumes about every Jew's identity.

My first husband was not Jewish, and it was a stumbling block in our relationship, among many. I noticed it in the subtle ways in which his mother and sister would merely tolerate me as a member of their family. Its presence was even greater in my family's grudging acceptance of him. Most of all, his family didn't quite "get" me, and mine definitely didn't "dig" him.

Suffice it to say, finding a Jewish man was important, if not absolutely necessary.

What about him having to be from New York? I do have several relatives from New York, including Dad. And my mother, a native Southern Californian, had always fancied herself an east coast sort. Essentially, Mom was a New Yorker wannabe.

But I have never lived anywhere other than So Cal. So, what gives?

Again, there's a certain sensibility. Although I lived in the Los Angeles area from birth until age 61, I'd often been mistaken for a New Yorker. I'm pretty sure this assessment resulted from my natural propensity to be impatient, direct, stylish and highly assertive. I possessed a personality that, until a few years ago, characterized relatively few among the So Cal population. I had little use for the typical laid-back, mellowed-out Californian.

You must know the California stereotype – those mumbly-mouthed surfer dudes who sound like they've just smoked a joint, and who wander through life thinking everything's just groovy, man.

Okay, so this is a considerable exaggeration when applied to the So Cal population at large. But as I cultivated my type A mentality, I became increasingly annoyed by my fellow Angeleno's. It seemed as though every time I got irritated over some trivial affront to my sense of urgency, someone would tell me to relax or chill out. No one seemed to understand, and there was certainly no one willing to commiserate. I came to mildly loathe those with whom I had occupied a major American city my entire life.

In contrast to this, I will never forget an incident that occurred on the first day of my very first trip to New York City. I was on a train into the city from upstate New York. We came to a station at which another train was supposed to have taken on some of the passengers from our train.

Our conductor spoke succinctly to us over the PA system.

His New York accent in full animation, the conductor announced, "The 'city train,' which just left this station less than a minute ago, was supposed to take on some of our passengers. But that train couldn't be bothered to wait an additional thirty seconds for us to arrive. Therefore, this train, an 'express train,' must now become a 'city train,' which means we will make *every single stop* on our way into New York City. Consequently, your arrival in the city will be delayed *a full hour and fifteen minutes*. The number to call to complain is…"

I couldn't believe my ears. I felt so validated in a way I'd never felt supported before. I was so grateful to finally, for the first time ever, have someone anticipate my aggravation in advance of it happening, thereby diffusing it before it had a chance to manifest. Not to mention, this conductor seemed sincerely frustrated for his passengers.

It was as if I'd come home. I felt an instant kinship with a man I'd never met before, and a place I'd never *been* before. This conductor was me, his psyche a veritable match to my own. I had found a kindred spirit, a soul mate in a man three thousand miles away from Los Angeles. And I had just arrived!

I thought, there must be thousands like this conductor here in New York City. I'd never met even one such individual in L.A. This is the kind of person I wanted to be around, not those who would have me "chill out."

There was more to this New York mindset. Recall my mentioning Dad had played handball at the Hollywood YMCA with a bunch of Jewish and Italian guys from New York. There was a manliness in the wearing of boxer shorts and athletic shirts (the ones commonly referred to as "wife beaters"). And although I certainly didn't want to marry a man like Dad, there was something about those boxer shorts and athletic shirts, and the distinctive and not-at-all-unpleasant gymnasium smell, that exuded an authentic masculine physicality.

Yes, my future mate should be from New York.

On expressing my desires in earnest to Mindy on that fateful day, I had simply thrown in the part about my fantasy man being named Sam. Since the character in the movie was called Sam, it seemed appropriate to include it for emphasis.

So, I had told Mindy I wanted to meet a man like the one in *Crossing Delancey*.

To my surprise, Mindy responded, "Oh, I know one. I work with him at the airline."

"You do?" I asked with interest… and *surprise*. "He's nice?"

"Yeah, he's *really* nice."

"Jewish?"

"Yep."

"From New York?"

"Yep."

"He's available?"

"Yeah, I'm pretty sure."

"What's his name?" I asked.

"Sam!"

"You're kidding."

"Nope."

"Huh. Do you think he'd like to meet someone like me?" I asked hopefully.

Mindy thought that, yes, he might like to meet me. She would tell him about me.

A couple of weeks later, Mindy's Sam finally called me. I immediately liked him over the phone. We seemed to have a lot to talk about. He also sounded very kind.

Our first date, a blind date, was on a Sunday afternoon. I watched out the window as Sam approached my front door. He was very nice looking, and I liked his shirt. It was long-sleeved, button-down, of a waffle weave fabric in sky blue.

That day Sam and I walked through some neighborhoods and the main commercial district of the trendy Belmont Shore area of Long Beach, where I'd been living for a few years. After a lovely Italian dinner, we walked past a video store with a rack of used VHS tapes on the sidewalk in front of the shop.

With a curious expression, Sam said, "Let's stop here a minute. I've been looking for something."

"Oh, what?" I asked.

You won't believe Sam's response. But I swear it's true.

Sam replied, "An obscure Jewish romance called *Crossing Delancey*."

Initially mortified, I blurted, "Mindy *told* you?!"

"Told me what?" Sam asked, obviously wondering why I'd suddenly become agitated.

I hadn't intended on telling Sam about my revelation to Mindy concerning the man I sought to meet. Not until at least a few dates hence, and obviously only if we continued seeing each other. But under the circumstances, I was forced to spill it all on our first date. And Mindy, it turned out, had not said a word to Sam about the "order I'd placed" for a man just like the one in the movie. It was all just a miraculous coincidence.

Wouldn't you know, my Sam turned out to be a type B New Yorker. Go figure. By personal preference, however, he intentionally eliminated his Brooklyn accent years ago. (The accent would re-emerge whenever Sam got angry with me. My delight in pointing out the fact generally put an immediate end to the argument.)

In keeping with my fond imaginings concerning men from New York, Sam did wear those boxer shorts and athletic shirts, just like the ones Dad wore at the Hollywood Y. Sam really was a New Yorker through and through, although the manifestations of it were subtle and sometimes hard to pin down.

On our second date, Sam brought me flowers and a jar of pickles. We were married a little over two years later.

Chapter Six
On Quasi-Perfectionism

Better a diamond with a flaw than a pebble without.
— Confucius

Quasi-perfectionism or *perfectionism?* Call it what you like. It seems to me *perfectionism* is the more extreme version. And let's face it, I am always looking for ways to think of myself as *less extreme*. So, please indulge me.

We are at long last getting to the stories with which, I trust, all type A's can identify. I am deeply grateful for your confidence in the process and hope you read earlier chapters from an analytical perspective. Perhaps you even shed a tear or two.

On to "quasi-perfectionism," the very essence of what it means to be type A. With quasi-perfectionism, "speed bumps" are inevitable.

What is a "quasi-perfectionist"?

FULL DISCLOSURE: I made up the term. And I will attempt to clarify its meaning.

Best defined by example, I think, it is someone who is perhaps a *neat* freak, but not a *clean* freak. It is a person who embarrasses herself ordering her daily latte (so many instructions, you see), but makes her menu selection without special requests when accompanying you to any restaurant.

A hoarder's clutter, if confined to another's space, though *bothersome* to her, is not nearly as devastating as a towel left unfolded in her own bathroom.

If allowed to progress to the toxic stage, the quasi-perfectionist might begin to hold others to unreasonable, even impossible, standards. The result is a fairly constant state of dashed expectations, disappointment, and *disdain*.

Harmless Quasi-Perfectionism

"What can I get for you?" asks the cheerful young woman at the register.

Knowing my order by rote from having repeated it many times, I place it without hesitation, "A Grande three-pump mocha, please, with one caffeinated shot and one decaf. I'd like it a hundred and seventy degrees with two percent milk and a standard amount of whipped cream."

Out of self-consciousness, I speak as softly as possible without rendering my conspicuously lengthy order inaudible. The last thing I'd want is to have to repeat it!

I intentionally stand right next to the pick-up counter waiting for my drink, hoping my attentiveness will prevent "the call-out."

No such luck.

It's always the same. Aware of my presence at the pick-up counter, where I am positioned for ready retrieval of my mocha while making eye contact with him or her, the habit-driven and conscientious barista loudly bares my finicky nature to all in proximity.

"One Grande half-caff three-pump two-percent extra-hot with-whip mocha for *Vi-i-i-i-cki-i-i-i-i!*"

Sometimes I've politely joked, "Shhh… my order's so long it's embarrassing."

Only to be told mine is nothing compared to some others.

I had the cute, but apparently insufferable (according to his coworkers), manager of one Starbucks go on to prove it by rapidly reeling off an order so long I was dizzy when he'd finished. The other employees were not amused, and made me pinky-swear never to get him started again.

After all this, at least I know my mocha will very likely turn out just the way I like it. An equitable trade-off – my reputation as a rational human being for the perfect mocha. I'm okay with that.

Truth be told, however, it's no fun being a fusspot. It drains one's energy, turning a person's attention and able intellect away from things consequential in favor of what can only be described as trivial. There simply isn't room in the brain or time in the day for both.

I am truly a prisoner of my own quasi-perfectionism. It's no laughing matter. Other quasi's will relate and they will empathize from the very cores of their beings. For this is not a chosen path. I'm convinced it comes about in one of two ways:

1) It is as inborn as being double-jointed or tone-deaf.

OR...

2) It is the natural response to parental control so deftly and covertly employed as to remain undiscovered for years, decades, perhaps even for life.

Early Manifestations of My Quasi-Perfectionism

I can attest to the fact I have needed for certain things to be "just so" as far back into early childhood as I can remember.

For example, my bedroom...

My best friend Carol had invited me over. We were in the third grade, and Carol lived in the hills in a pristine upscale tract of brand spanking new 1960's homes with white rock roofs, sliding glass doors in extruded aluminum frames, "high tech" kitchens featuring built-in dishwashers, and kidney-shaped swimming pools with bright blue chlorinated water. There was shag carpeting in almost every uncluttered room, an open-air terrarium in the ceramic tiled entry, and a slim-line phone in her parents' enormous bedroom.

Compared to our 1930's streamline Moderne home, Carol's house was a palace. I loved going over there.

Carol's bedroom was far from messy. The bed was made, and nothing was strewn about the carpeted floor. But my eye caught the pillow sham on her bed. It was not aligned properly with the pattern in Carol's bedspread. There was no artistic flare to its skewed positioning. It had clearly been laid on the bed carelessly and with no thought given to the aesthetics of its placement. Carol's desk and dresser were in the same perilous condition. My disapproval remained my secret.

My bedroom? Frankly, it was a neat freak's paradise. I cannot recall a single time when my mother told me to clean up my room. I can, however, remember more than one occasion when Mom begged me, to no avail, to leave my bed unmade for a few minutes and come to breakfast before my over-easy eggs got cold. Or to hang up my freshly laundered clothes *after* dinner.

"Please?!" she would beseech me.

It was no use. I simply couldn't comply. I was driven.

I believe a *true,* rather than *quasi-,* perfectionist would avoid *all* clutter. That wasn't me. Growing up, I had some fifteen stuffed animals occupying the surface of my twin-size bed during all waking hours. And each one sat atop the very same square inches of bedspread it had resided on the day before… and the day before that… and the day before that.

I took great care to design my stuffed animal display for optimum visual appeal. If and when a new stuffed pet joined the menagerie, the entire arrangement might well be contrived anew to avoid any possibility of observable imbalance.

So, just how strong was this compulsion?

Sadly, I was a slave to it. If a friend came over, she would invariably notice something of interest on my dresser – a piece of jewelry, a figurine, or some other tchotchke. Naturally, she would pick up the coveted item, admire it, and place it back down.

Of course, the well-meaning friend's return of the item to the surface of my dresser never quite duplicated the exact orientation of the item prior to its momentary removal. It would be slightly rotated from its precisely "calculated" original angle, or placed a few centimeters from its well-considered usual coordinates, or both.

My dilemma was this: Would it be worth the humiliation of picking up the object then and there, with my friend still present, and returning it to its arbitrarily established "correct" positioning on the dresser, thus delivering me from temporary high anxiety? Or could I possibly force myself to leave the item displaced until the friend left, thereby preserving my reputation as a normal kid?

What do you think?

You guessed it. I couldn't wait. I would return the item to its proper placement immediately.

Quasi-Perfectionist "Pet Peeves"

What exactly is a "pet peeve"?

I define the phenomenon as a usually minor, but could be major, annoyance. It seems to crop up over and over again as we travel through life. It is often predictable and always irritating.

The resulting exasperation doesn't seem to lessen with each passing episode of the offending incident. Rather, the peeved individual develops an increasing intolerance for future occurrences. She grows weary and resigned, but the peeve itself endures. It persists in its aggravation like a sore that never heals, or a splinter her tweezers won't reach.

I would guess everyone has pet peeves. I would also venture to say some personality types are more susceptible than others.

Enter once again the type A quasi-perfectionist. If there is any human being more likely than the type A quasi to suffer from hyper-sensitivity to the pet peeve, I would love to know who it might be.

The type A quasi, with her renowned impatience and tendency to want and expect things to be a particular way, would certainly possess numerous pet peeves. Just for fun, let's look at some of my "favorites":

No. 1 Weak Decaffeinated Coffee

Have you ever wondered why decaffeinated coffee ordered in a restaurant is usually weaker than the regular? Such a question would never have occurred to you? Well, it has occurred to me on many occasions.

I suppose the natural assumption of restaurant personnel, especially if not themselves connoisseurs of excellent coffee, would be that people who don't want the caffeine really don't like coffee very much. Hence, the average decaf drinker would appreciate a weaker cup.

It also costs less to make weak coffee, so why waste perfectly good coffee beans on a customer who will likely grimace at the taste of a bold brew?

This analysis probably sounds very reasonable to many. It does not, however, make the slightest bit of sense to the devoted decaf drinker. In fact, this argument is inherently illogical, and I will demonstrate why.

First of all, coffee isn't the only game in town. If a person doesn't care much for the taste of coffee, they probably won't order it. They will opt for hot tea or iced tea or Dr. Pepper or a Coke. They might even go for lemonade or hot cocoa or a New York egg cream. The one thing they won't order is coffee – decaf or otherwise.

Second, most decaf drinkers have a reason for drinking decaf and not regular. Their rationale surely has *nothing whatsoever* to do with a preference for weak coffee.

Many people are highly sensitive to caffeine. It may cause them frightening heart palpitations, monthly breast tenderness, heightened anxiety or sleepless nights. These folks do themselves a grave disservice to consume significant quantities of caffeine.

Third, and here's the clincher, since the decaf coffee drinker doesn't get to experience the delight of caffeine's buzz, and since she can't depend on a cup o' joe to jump-start her engine in the morning, why in the world would she even bother stopping in at her local diner, donut shop or coffee house to buy a cup of decaf?

There is only one reasonable explanation for why the decaf drinker drinks decaf. ***The decaf devotee truly loves the taste of coffee.***

This means she undoubtedly craves her brew bold and strong. It's the only answer that makes sense, and it should be obvious.

So, number one, first and foremost, topping my list of pet peeves is weak decaf.

How irrational. Utterly disheartening. So dumb. Simply unacceptable.

No. 2 Lemon slices as a replacement for lemon wedges

This is a relatively recent phenomenon, which makes it especially sad.

I'm fond of ordering a big glass of iced tea when out for lunch. In the warmer months there is simply nothing better.

I never sweeten my beverages and always ask for an additional lemon wedge or two for my iced tea. The extra wedges will be needed for refills, and I will certainly consume two or three.

Whereas lemon *wedges* used to be de rigueur with iced tea, now almost all establishments provide lemon *half-slices*. Even most upscale restaurants have made this unfortunate switch.

My extra lemons always arrive, but they are in the form of *half-slices*, in spite of my having specified *wedges*.

"What's the difference?" you ask.

"Gosh, you're fussy," you opine.

Given you had to ask and opine, I already know you are not an imbiber of iced tea with lemon. If you were, the answer would be self-evident.

The lemon wedge has enough rigidity and peel surface that, when grasped for squeezing, it yields the desired amount of lemon juice into the tea without making a mess.

The lemon half-slice, on the other hand, is thin and wobbly. There is insufficient peel surface for handling without one's fingers making abundant contact with the lemon flesh. Squeezing cannot be accomplished with any degree of control. And once you have completed the task, your fingers are covered with lemon juice.

Are you convinced?

I'll take your silence as a yes.

No. 3 Ice Cream Cone Etiquette Part A – those dumb "glued"-on cone wrappers

If I have commuted via L.A.'s Metro Rail to get to and from work, chances are it has been a long day. Furthermore, I may have had to put up with the attitude of several foul-mouthed teenagers, the stench of one or more unbathed homeless persons, and/or the proselytizing of someone marginally sane and taking advantage of a captive audience.

After all that, I may feel I deserve a treat – an ice cream cone. Happily, the ice cream store is on my way home from the train station. I will stop for a "kid's scoop," and the stress and slight motion sickness from the train will all melt away. (No pun intended.)

My "kid's scoop," a smaller version of a single scoop, will sit atop a sugar cone ensconced in a specially designed conical paper wrapper. The wrapper is "glued" to the cone using some sort of edible adhesive.

I hate these paper wrappers with a passion and seek to immediately remove the offending membrane before commencing my enjoyment of the treat. The employees at my local store have observed this little routine. They discretely give each other the fish-eye and think I don't notice.

When I was a kid, this ice cream chain's employees would wrap each cone on the spot with a plain piece of thin wax paper. There was no adhesive involved. The customer was simply trusted to grasp the wrapped cone using the proper force so the cone would not eject from the wrapper and land scoop-first on the floor. It never happened to me, at any rate, and I was six years old when Mom started taking Bobby and me for an ice cream cone once a week after school.

With the dumbed-down "glued"-on paper wrappers of today, please tell me what is intended to happen when the customer has consumed the ice cream down to the cone and now wishes to eat the cone? She must fumble to remove the paper, thereby interrupting her ice cream enjoyment, in order to bite into the cone without also ingesting the wrapper.

I simply refuse. This is why I take care of the problem at the outset, before I even start to lick away at my ice cream. This way I can enjoy my treat, start to finish, uninterrupted.

No. 4 Ice Cream Cone Etiquette Part B – soft ice cream

Note: *When I say "soft ice cream," I do not mean soft serve, which I rather like. I am talking about regular ice cream served when at a less-than-optimal state of hardness.*

I think soft ice cream is just icky. But okay, I will admit this one is a matter of personal taste. Still, if you are having your scoop on a cone, soft ice cream is a major mess unless you eat it fast, mighty fast. This won't do.

I don't want to rush my ice cream treat. Furthermore, there is something about licking a rock-hard scoop that results in just the right quantity of ice cream transferring to the tongue. For me, it is very satisfying. Never mind, the poor guy or girl serving me will be getting that week's upper body workout just from scooping my ice cream.

When ordering my kid's scoop on a sugar cone, I may well ask whether my chosen flavor is soft or hard. If my server says it is soft, I will make another selection. From experience, I have come to know Mint Chip can almost always be depended upon to be nice and firm. Fortunately, Mint Chip is a flavor I particularly like.

Problem pretty much solved, unless I happen to be in the mood for Coffee or Rocky Road. In this case, all bets are off and I will have to request a taste to avoid catastrophe.

"Here comes that kooky lady who will interrogate us as to which flavors are hard, and who refuses to leave the wrapper on the cone," is a sentiment I imagine has been expressed more than once by employees of my local ice cream store upon my approach.

This is precisely why I haven't dared to make an issue of my biggest ice cream pet peeve of all...

No. 5 Ice Cream Cone Etiquette Part C – paying after being handed the cone

That pretty much says it. But I will elucidate.

Her ice cream cone has been scooped and is ready to be enjoyed. Except for one thing. She now has to pay for it.

Prior to the ice cream cone being scooped, both her hands were free to take money out of her wallet and to place her change back in the wallet.

Once one hand is holding her ice cream cone, the task of paying for the treat becomes significantly more difficult to accomplish. She manages to "single-handedly" make the payment, but she ponders why it was necessary for her to develop this skill in the first place.

Things get even more maddening if the ice cream store employee helping her must wait for access to the cash register. There the poor customer stands having to start eating her ice cream cone to prevent it from melting while payment is delayed.

I really hate when that happens.

If only payment could be made before her ice cream is scooped. But alas, it's too logical. It would never catch on.

As you might imagine, I could name more of these offending annoyances. But most of my other pet peeves are so common they are hardly worthy of mention, much less of elaboration. Some of them are:

- a child who screams in a restaurant, and whose parents do nothing to stop it, appearing to think it's enchanting and cute
- being placed on hold by an automated phone system, with no indication as to whether I will remain on hold for two minutes or two hours
- automated phone systems in general
- a motorist travelling well below the posted speed limit while driving in the *left lane* (more on this in Chapter 11: Road Rage 101)
- *literal* speed bumps (again, see Chapter 11)
- an otherwise courteous person yakking away on a cell phone as she, in her distraction, lets the door she has just opened for herself slam in the face of the innocent soul who follows behind her

So, I ask you, who is the greater fool – the perpetrator of the behavior resulting in another's pet peeve, or the peeved? A question for the ages.

The Quasi-Perfectionist Reader

How do you suppose a quasi-perfectionist would go about reading a book?

To the quasi-perfectionist, a book can be an enormous obligation. And the longer the tome the greater the burden. This is because quasi-perfectionists don't read parts of books. They are compelled to read the whole thing.

This particular quasi will readily make exception for textbooks, in which portions are assigned, and other parts can perhaps be trusted to be irrelevant to the topic being taught in class.

My husband Sam would read parts of books and had no qualms about telling people he read those books. He wouldn't qualify his response by explaining he'd read certain chapters or sections of the work in question. He just said he'd read it. This is true even if he'd spent only a half hour skimming the book! How his good-as-gold conscience justified this deception is unfathomable to my quasi-perfectionist sensibilities.

If I were to tell someone I read a book I hadn't completed cover-to-cover, I don't think I could live with the guilt. And what of the anxiety? Suppose, in discussing the book with someone who had read it, the person asked for my take on a chapter I hadn't read?! Oh boy.

So why doesn't the quasi just read part of a book and say so?

She can't. She would always wonder if she had missed a section that made sense of the book's message. She would worry that, in reading only a portion, she had irresponsibly caused herself to be misled. After all, we know what can happen when we don't get the whole story...

Most of all, she would know she'd exerted a significant amount of effort into a "job" she hadn't finished. It would seem a waste.

So, reading a book is a project for the quasi. She must temporarily alter her lifestyle to get through it. Once she has completed the task, she feels triumphant, and breathes a big sigh of relief.

I recently read a 400-page book written by one of my favorite radio talk show hosts. The first half of the book was quite different from the second half. The initial 200-or-so pages were laugh-out-loud entertaining, whereas the latter portion was more serious, less packed with life lessons, and a tougher read overall.

This book was an excellent candidate for a partial read. But it would never happen. Not on my turf. Not in a million years.

Consequently, the quasi must take great care not to enter casually into additional magazine subscriptions. Each one could well represent an intolerable time commitment.

I once subscribed to a magazine whose theme was the preservation of historically significant architecture. My interest in the publication spoke to an uncharacteristic activist passion in me. At around the same time I maintained a subscription to a figure skating magazine, which I fondly called "my bi-monthly brain candy." Hey, I was a skating fan. We all have our eccentricities.

Fortunately, both of these periodicals came out only six times per year. Needless to say, I devoured each of them once every two months, *cover to cover*.

I followed this rule with such devotion, I once let a professional society membership lapse to release me from having to fully digest the organization's monthly news edition. (Kidding.)

Okay, I joked about not renewing the membership. But you get the point.

And what of all the newsletters from financial institutions, investment funds, and health organizations, not to mention the various informational inserts from our employers, our utility providers, and the communities in which we live?

Thank goodness, I drew the line at those. Can you imagine if I hadn't?

As you can see, the quasi-perfectionist reader is a very responsible individual.

The Quasi-Perfectionist Writer

I have always been told the correct way to write something of any significant length is to get the thoughts down as quickly as possible and perfect it later. It's called "freewriting" or "brainstorming," among other monickers. After all of the ideas are down on paper, there is a first draft, second draft, etc.

In school this method was drilled into us. I've also read about it and talked to other writers, all of whom will verify the technique's undeniable validity.

Knowing what you now know about the quasi-perfectionist, do you think there is any possibility whatsoever that this poor up-tight soul could possibly make use of this time-tested and well-established process? Of course not.

The quasi-perfectionist scribe perfects as she goes. The procedure may seem laborious to others. But it satisfies her need to avoid all semblance, however temporary, of bad grammar and poor composition, as well as the utterly unacceptable spelling and typographical errors that would surely ensue. And when she is at long last finished, there are no second or third drafts to write. Her well-contrived piece requires only minor changes to improve a sentence here or there for maximum reader impact.

I love writing this way. I know it is universally considered all wrong. But it works for me.

My friend William and I were both theater critics in the city in which Sam and I once lived. William is a highly creative writer who gives little thought to sentence length or structure. He is decidedly not a perfectionist, quasi- or otherwise.

I too, believe it or not, took fairly sizable liberties when writing theater reviews. If done right, a review written with artful imperfections is freeing, fun, and pretty well accepted in the world of "critique journalism," generally speaking.

But William told me he knocks out a review in about twenty minutes. I believe him. He doesn't worry about making the review better. He goes with his first instinct and calls it a day.

I, on the other hand, agonize long and hard over my opening. From there, the rest comes easily, or not. In the end, I have done my best to strike a tone, be it amusing, intellectual, clever, or any combination of the three. I have probably spent an hour and a half.

Often I liked my review as much or more than the one written by William. But there were times when I concluded his was the superior piece – William's, the writing of which took roughly one quarter the time I spent on mine.

I think it's all about letting go, something the need-to-be-in-control quasi-perfectionist finds exceedingly difficult.

The Quasi-Perfectionist Party Host

Entertaining at home is yet another monumental undertaking to the type A quasi. After all, if everything isn't exactly right, she might never forgive herself. At the very least, her shame would haunt her for weeks, maybe months.

Hence, she organizes the minutest detail to the nth degree, and she does this even for a casual card game or movie night.

Prior to a gathering, she attempts to predict every possible misstep, making advance provision for each potential issue's remedy, just in case.

The type A party host is nervous leading up to her guests' arrival, mentally berating herself for what she perceives is her inability to put on a fun and people-pleasing get-together. All this, even though every party she's ever thrown has been a huge success.

And what about the elements of unexpected "chaos" she has no ability to prevent?

These show up in the form of coolers and paper bags placed on her countertop or floor, items producing a visual distraction amidst her perfectly-planned food and beverage display.

When no one is watching, she quietly throws the "debris" into the pantry in order to rid the environment of unnecessary clutter.

Years ago, I hosted a brunch with many family members and friends in attendance. Everything was ready to go when my guests arrived. Food and beverage items were all set out in accordance with my thoughtfully-designed arrangement. Dishes were done, the sink completely clean and clear. The coffee maker was set to brew at the flip of a switch. I was thrilled to begin the party with everything in perfect order.

Guests began to arrive. A friend of my mother's came with a lovely breakfast casserole I hadn't known she'd be bringing.

I tried to be gracious in light of her generosity. But to my type A quasi-perfectionist mind-set, gratitude was the furthest thing from my mind. Frankly, I resented the introduction of an additional dish my brunch buffet didn't need. I viewed it as an imbalance to my well-thought-out menu.

To add insult to injury, Mom's friend told me the casserole needed to be heated. But I had my own breakfast torte in the oven, and scones awaiting their turn to bake. Deep down I was furious, as heating the casserole would upset the timing of my meal. Needless to say, I'd worked out the oven schedule to the minute so everything could be served hot.

Of course, we managed to pull off a fine brunch in spite of the "hiccup." And this is exactly the point.

A type B party host always takes a "the more the merrier" attitude toward any unforeseen addition, be it unanticipated guests or extra food. She doesn't care if people place bags, containers, utensils, purses, jackets, etc. all over her counters and floor.

Her thought is, *no one cares.* And no one does.

It's taken me years of entertaining to lighten up just a smidge. Closely observing the party hosting habits of my type B friends has helped a lot. Thank heaven for the type B's!

The Quasi-Perfectionist Driver

See Chapter 11: Road Rage 101

At the Toxic Level

Perhaps the most dishonorable manifestation of my quasi-perfectionism was the growing tendency to project it onto others. Sometime in my mid-20s, I noted in myself an inclination to judge others harshly. I suppose it was a form of self-validation. But I was validating the worst of myself, not the best.

I illogically reasoned, "If I can do it, so can they." (And if they didn't, they had something gravely wrong with them.)

In other words, if it was in my skill set, it should also be in theirs.

What?

Of course I knew it wasn't true. I knew everyone has his own aptitudes and failings. And as you can see, I'm perfectly willing to poke fun at my own flawed persona.

Even so, I spent my 30s refining a type A personality of the highest order, unaware of the slippery slope awaiting me.

As a mechanical equipment applications engineer, I turned out work of exceptional quality and lots of it. Having been a top-notch student of English grammar and a first-rate natural speller, I was able to produce well-written correspondence, quotations and specifications with no spelling nor grammatical errors whatsoever.

It became clear to me that a good mastery of the English language was an increasingly rare phenomenon among the American working populace, and even rarer among engineers like myself. So, my work quality was a source of great pride. I was certain it would set me apart. As my company's employee, I would stand out in the best possible way.

In addition, if the requests for assistance with equipment selection or specification were especially prolific at work on a given day, I simply worked faster to keep up. I was a dynamo of quasi-perfectionist productivity – a veritable "God's gift" to my employer.

The problem was, I grew to loathe those who couldn't measure up to my impossible standard. Never mind the fact there were countless areas of life in which my abilities didn't live up to the fine example set by others.

Still, I persisted. If I happened to pluck a paper off the fax machine – a page riddled with the usual spelling mistakes, poor grammar, and typographical errors – my judgmental disgust at the perpetrator shifted into high gear. If the creator of the document were a co-worker, I might make a passive-aggressive snide comment as I "charitably" delivered the page(s) to the unfortunate individual.

If the author were a customer of ours, the offense would be neatly filed in the ready recesses of my memory as part of an on-going tally, which might build to the point of payback at some future date.

Worse yet, the examples of rampant imperfection began to pervade every nook and cranny of office life. And once email took our lives by storm, so did an unbelievably annoying affront to the written word – the new, hip and cool, *completely unpunctuated* email message. (Major groan.)

Even my boss' boss would send out emails containing nary a comma, nor period, *nor capitalized proper noun.*

They may as well have poisoned my coffee the day this trend started. It would have saved me the pain of having to grow accustomed to this careless, dumbed-down, error-strewn, stream-of-consciousness insult to everyday communication.

I viewed it as *sanctioned illiteracy.*

The point is, the work ethic I embodied, and that I was certain represented the best any employee could offer an employer, was quickly going the way of the Triceratops. And I was developing into a nightmare of impatience and contempt disguised as my version of excellent customer service.

Well, one day the inevitable happened. My employer found out.

What I didn't realize then was that some work environments are more consistently irritating than others. If I had, I may have changed careers long before I did.

In my line of work at the time, the customers were mainly commercial new construction sub-contractors and design engineers. With the exception of a few particularly well-organized individuals, this group exemplified all things aggravating to me. They lost faxes I'd sent them only moments earlier. They would forget to place an order and then require the item tomorrow. They routinely let their accounts lapse for nonpayment. The letters, faxes, requests for proposal, and purchase orders they sent us were fraught with careless errors of every conceivable kind. I could go on and on, but you get the idea.

All these things and more turned my otherwise manageable job into a high-stress carousel of jumping through hoops and putting out fires, often to find out the hoop jumping and fire "extinguishing" had been unnecessary after all.

What had been an emergency yesterday had overnight morphed into, "Oh yeah, turns out we don't need it till next month."

The non-quasi, often in the form of the type B personality, takes these things in stride. This individual works at one speed, no matter the crisis. They do the best they can without ever excreting a gram of adrenalin.

From behind the "bars" of my type A quasi-perfectionist "prison cell," however, I could only observe this phenomenon with profound disapproval at what seemed to me a complete failure to respond to urgency.

With all this annoyance pushing my now hyper-sensitive buttons, and without much break in the action, my scorn snowballed into a pressure-cooker of disrespect.

Oh, I was no dummy. I struggled hard to balance the negativity with charm and friendliness. I was even fairly successful at it for quite a while. But the seismic pressure inside my volcano was building. It was only a matter of time until I would go too far with one of our customers.

Disaster, it turns out, came in the form of a fairly benign comment to the wrong guy at the wrong time.

In yet another instance of a lost fax, and could I please send it again, I felt justified in taking mild exception to the old cliche, "the customer's always right."

In a joking tone, I offered the culprit, "You guys must have a little mouse over there that eats faxes."

How harmful could that remark be? And it would relieve some of my frustration, so it's the perfect remedy for all concerned, right?

Wrong. The boss got a call from the customer later that day and called me into her office to tell me about it. It would be the first of several sessions in which my out-of-control behavior would be at issue.

Suffice it to say, my quasi-perfectionism-induced actions cost me at least one promotion. And perhaps even more demoralizing, God's gift to my employer (that's me, remember) came to be appreciated solely for what my boss described as producing "high volume."

High volume! That's merely *quantity!* What about the thorough and on-time specifications and quotations? What about the perfect grammar, spelling, and composition with no typos? Is it possible no one had noticed the superior *quality* of my work? Can it be that all of my skill and organization – indeed my quasi-perfectionism – had been perceived as, and reduced to, nothing more than my willingness to work like a chicken with its head cut off?

Yes, it is more than possible. It hit me like a ton of bricks. Most managers in today's workplace don't value a well-written document because *they don't recognize it when they see it.* And they don't recognize it because they themselves rose to their elevated positions without ever having been expected to produce such a document.

The very thing I valued most in myself as an employee was virtually worthless in today's workplace.

So, I asked myself, should I give up and settle into mediocrity because I'm only good at things people no longer give a rip about? Or should I view this as an opportunity to learn from my mistakes?

I thought, perhaps I could find a work environment offering some breathing room between lesser, and less frequent, frustrations. Theoretically, this should prevent the slow but constant rise in pressure within Mount Vicki.

Furthermore, I could build upon my skills with a greater degree of outward focus. This might involve pursuing on-the-job tasks with a priority given to making my boss look as good as possible.

Hmmm, what a concept.

Survivor that I am, I accepted the challenge I'd presented to myself. Better late than never, and with a little help from serendipity, I found the niche I was looking for.

Chapter Seven
Desperately Seeking Validation

Determination becomes obsession – and then it becomes all that matters. – Jeremy Irvine

This true story illustrates my type A persona on steroids. No embellishments were added.

Resolved to achieve career success on my own terms, I went for it as only a type A could. When "speed bumps" got in the way, I tackled each one like a warrior goddess who'd never lost in battle... and never would.

In short, defeat was not an option.

Having spent the first sixty percent of my career in the private sector, I'd always assumed government work to be a sorry step-child – indeed, the Cinderella of employment options. After all, private companies offered better compensation, more challenging work, and more upward mobility, right? And an employee with such a company could feel proud to be a member of the superior class of workers who hadn't had to settle for that last-resort option – *working for the government.*

I suppose I ought to excuse my own ignorance by acknowledging a scarcely noticeable shift occurring sometime during the 1990s in which government employment became the place to be, especially in terms of compensation. This transition ostensibly emanated from the increased unionization of public sector employees, coupled with a growing symbiosis between those unions and the public officials they seek to elect. All of this came at the expense of the taxpayers, who mostly work in the private sector.

An unsavory state of affairs? Yes, in my opinion. The jobs? Well, someone has to do them.

In any case, it had taken me twenty years to learn how to be an employee any employer would covet. Mind you, I still didn't recognize the value of government employment per se, but was more than open to it out of a need – no, a *desperation* – to leave my career as an applications engineer.

Make no mistake, over all it had been a highly satisfying run, packed with opportunities, successes and valuable lessons learned. But sadly, it ended with a company and a situation from which I couldn't wait to get away, a very long distance away. Pride swallowed, I wanted only the chance to start fresh.

The odd thing was, my dad had made a successful white-collar career with the government and had thoroughly enjoyed it. But Dad was such an off-beat character, no one put much stock in what he thought of things. And it wasn't his way to attempt to exert much influence.

Still, it took one final job change, and a disastrous one, to prompt my flight from applications engineering and the private sector.

My new employer had promised an outstanding product line, solid technical and financial backing for the satellite office I would be helping to run, and honest business practices.

He lied. Or maybe he was lying to himself more than to me.

Carl was the oddest duck I'd ever worked with. When I first met him, he appeared so normal and decent – a real regular guy. But inside of a couple of months, unpleasant things began to come to light. The first clue should have been the sudden departure of the other engineer in my office the very week I started.

On his way out, my short-time cohort Bill said he hadn't wanted to alarm me. He suggested Carl wasn't the good guy he appeared. Bill refused to go into detail.

Not wishing to react to incomplete second-hand information from someone I barely knew, I put Bill's warnings aside and proceeded to learn the product lines and engineer the systems we represented. I even brought in my friend Tori to be our crackerjack new parts sales and clerical associate. Things were going swimmingly.

But our elation was short-lived. Tori and I started getting some really bad attitude whenever we called the main office in Northern California. We gradually realized the "attitude" who ran that office had some sort of an "in" with Carl.

We eventually became privy to the startling but illuminating news the "attitude" was indeed having an affair with Carl. Her uncooperative stance made our jobs difficult, and complaints to Carl, of course, fell on disinterested ears.

Then one of our primary manufacturers inexplicably dropped us as a distributor. Soon after losing the product line, our biggest customer stopped placing orders with us in favor of ordering from my once colleague Bill, who had moved on to replicate the most lucrative service we provided. When I queried the customer as to why they had switched suppliers, I was treated to a laundry list of grievances against the enigmatic Carl, including (what a surprise) his having repeatedly lied to them.

Manufacturers began refusing to ship product until the main office paid its bills. Others expressed low confidence in our company's ability to stay afloat. Tori and I started to wonder what the heck we'd gotten ourselves into.

This is where serendipity enters the picture. On a whim, Sam and I had been taking a weekly evening course in introductory real estate appraisal. Sam, who had signed onto the class because he didn't want me going to the college campus alone at night, wasn't much interested in the subject matter. I thought it was fascinating.

So, when things became untenable with my new employer, I paid a visit to the local office of the County assessor to see about a job as a real property appraiser. A nice appraiser took the time to speak with me, informing me the annual entry exam would be given in just a couple of weeks. I still had a few days to submit an application. What spectacular timing!

I made my application, was one of only about 60 applicants to pass the test, and earned a first interview and then a second. Out of some 700 initial applicants, I was offered one of the eighteen available spots in the next appraiser trainee class.

Yes!

Except, no. The starting pay would be far too low. How could I do that to Sam? How could I justify it to myself?

But Sam had an instinct about this. He felt it was the opportunity I'd been searching for, and he was adamant I take the job if I wanted it. We would get by, he insisted. Thank goodness I listened to him.

I will never forget Carl's words when I gave him my two weeks' notice:

"You're leaving this fantastic position to go to work for the *government?* What, are you *nuts?!*"

I didn't think so, not by a longshot, especially given the increasingly problematic environment at Carl's company. I left there with no misgivings whatsoever.

What about Tori, you wonder? She stayed on a while longer, affording me wonderful juicy stories (all right, gossip) about the ever-wackier goings on with Carl and the "attitude." Then, at the proper time, without missing a beat, she got a great job at a local college and ventured forth happy as a clam.

As for me, I've never looked back except out of immense gratitude for my good fortune.

Life as an appraiser for the Assessor is best appreciated by those of us who once worked for private businesses. Those who haven't had a full experience of the private sector tend to take their government employment, with its superior compensation and retirement packages, for granted.

But you're asking, "What about that world famous apathy characteristic of government workers?"

In my department, it was part truth and mostly myth. Don't forget, appraisal staff were pretty heavily weeded through in the selection process for employment. Eighteen trainees chosen out of 700 applicants, remember?

Oh, I won't try to tell you there were no bad apples. There were a few. But by and large, this work environment was a seventh heaven of varied assignments, lateral and upward mobility, and engaging co-workers.

What about the well-rumored government job stability? No rumor. For the most part, if one leaves the County it's because they choose to do so. Needless to say, most of those who opted to leave hadn't worked in the private sector. Some of those who left came back to rejoin our ranks a few "educational" months or years later.

In far rarer circumstances, an individual was fired for cause, having committed an act so egregious (downloading such an enormous quantity of material from porn sites as to jam the entire department's computer network is one example that comes to mind), even the countless layers of employee rights protection built into personnel policy couldn't save the poor foolish soul from termination.

So, why is it the government lifers didn't harbor the same appreciation and fondness for their jobs as those of us who came to government employment from the school of private sector hard knocks? It's like anything else. You can't fully realize the value in what you've got unless you've had something less. In this regard, I remain forever thankful for the "speed bumps" constituting the last two jobs from my prior career as an engineer.

There is nothing sweeter than the ability to appreciate your circumstances. Gratitude is hard-won, but worth every ounce of anguish in the struggle to attain it.

You are probably beginning to believe government employment may have its advantages. But you still remain skeptical, and rightly so. After all, no employment situation is without its lunacy. There will always be politics. Let me tell you about my own personal saga of sadness…

If you read the chapter on quasi-perfectionism, you know that under the right circumstances, and with all the stars in the cosmos optimally aligned, I can be, well, *driven*. This was precisely my state of mind as I embarked on my year-long adventure as a Real Property Appraiser Trainee.

Of course I was highly motivated. I was a type A individual of greater than average intelligence, with sparks here and there of savant-like ability. My best efforts had managed to achieve only a modicum of success during a twenty-two-year engineering career. Frankly, I had something to prove. It was now a case of do or die.

No, thoughts of suicide would not have reared their heads if this hadn't worked out. But I may well have one day come to the natural end of my life feeling as though I'd blown it.

The truth is, I felt badly in need of validation.

So, there I was on the first day of training, sitting with the other fourteen of what was now a total of fifteen appraiser trainees. Three of the chosen eighteen were no-shows. Perhaps, unlike Sam, they or their spouses hadn't so readily accepted the shockingly low starting salary.

Ranging in age from mid-20s to late 50s, we were a diverse group. Age-wise I fit comfortably into the middle of the pack.

On our first day, the Assessor, demonstrating what I thought was an exemplary display of good judgment and class, showed up with all of the department's top managers to meet and address the new trainees. Speaking to us one by one, the Assessor and other managers gave us our first inklings into the organization and opportunities available to us. We, of course, had much more to learn.

At the end of his rather no-nonsense speech, the one fairly intimidating manager of the group threw down the gauntlet. This was it, the inspiration I'd been hoping for.

The trainee who, at the end of the training year, graduated at the top of the class would get to choose the residential appraisal location he or she wanted to work in.

Okay, so the payoff wasn't an instant promotion or five-figure lump-sum bonus. Admittedly, I didn't care too much about choosing my eventual work location. We soon learned the department placed appraisers as close to home as possible.

No, what got me going was the manager's unspoken message, a meaning I astutely inferred from his challenge that day: *It mattered who graduated at the top of the class.*

It quickly became apparent which trainees were going to go for it. There were only three or four of us. The others clearly just wanted to make it through training.

There were subtle telling signs. For example, when our graded exams were returned to us, furtive glances from just a few of us attempted to discretely make out each other's scores. Or the subtly inquisitive remarks at break time to gain such information came from that same few, including (I'm so ashamed) myself. The competition was on, and may the best trainee win!

Honestly, it was neck and neck for the first nine months or so. Each of us "players" would score in the mid-to-high nineties on every exam. Each time a different one of us would get the highest score.

What separated the field in the end was a rather challenging project called the "narrative appraisal." This was a sixty- to seventy-page master work for which we were given ten Fridays to complete. It wasn't nearly enough.

Taking the assignment as seriously as one might imagine, I lived and breathed the thing for ten weeks. The Fridays were just the tip of the iceberg.

I quit my figure skating lessons and temporarily stopped reviewing plays for the paper. My publisher understood and generously offered her best wishes for my success.

I apologized in advance to Sam based on my expectation he would be almost entirely ignored for the better part of two months.

Upon completion, I turned out a narrative appraisal of such quality, recalling it still blows me away.

I assumed my competition would endow their "narratives" with the same amount of effort and care as I put into mine. Come to find out, they did not. With the exception of one other trainee who did a decent job on his narrative appraisal, my opponents turned out to be pretenders.

The project was simply too overwhelming for most of them. Some of them procrastinated, putting off the bulk of the work until a week or two before the due date. They used all those Fridays to lay out on the beach or go skiing in the local mountains.

At year's end, only nine of us finished training, some leaving by choice, others not making the cut. I got by far the highest score on the "narrative" and graduated at the top of the class. Sam was so proud.

I wasn't finished proving myself *to* myself, but I had overcome the first obstacle, achieved the first goal. I was rolling.

You may be wondering if my fellow trainees didn't find me a tad arrogant. I know some of them did. I was largely unaware of it at the time, because my past career "mistakes" made me feel so justified in trying extra hard to do my very best.

I would later count some of those same fellow trainees among my dearest friends. As for my intense drive, it was something my classmates didn't understand. How could they? After all, my real opponent in this game was my past self, and no one else.

They also didn't see that I am among the least devious of the inhabitants of this planet. I am as un-street smart as they come. What God giveth to me in spelling, writing, and mathematics ability, he taketh away in the realm of street savvy. And I'm just as happy to have it that way.

If any of my colleagues doubted my integrity, their distrust was completely misplaced. I would say this in earnest with my hand on a Mount Everest comprised entirely of bibles.

So, I became an appraiser assigned to the location nearest my home, which would have been the case regardless of my status at the top of the class.

In fact, graduating in the number one spot turned out to be a non-event. The manager who had thrown down the proverbial gauntlet didn't congratulate me until many months had passed. Frankly, I felt a little cheated. But this just kept me motivated to set myself apart in some other way.

Endeavoring to learn as much as possible as quickly as possible, I volunteered for every nasty appraisal assignment no one else wanted to tackle. I turned out to be less naturally talented as an appraiser than some others, including one or two of my classmates. Training was one thing; the real work environment was another. But I persisted in doing a good job, and my supervisors came to appreciate me for my willingness and dependability.

Recall this was just what I'd hoped to accomplish. I had vowed to pursue my new career with an emphasis on making my bosses look good. It really works!

When the time came for a few of us to volunteer to create in-house training sessions to benefit co-workers, one of the senior appraisers in my group thought I would be the perfect partner. She was right. I taught myself PowerPoint and put together our *two-hour* presentation. It turned out very well.

The following year, I proposed another in-house training session on a subject of my own choosing. The topic I selected, "Architectural Styles and Features," was readily accepted by the state organization governing our continuing education and certification program.

I was delighted, as I'd always wanted to learn about architecture but knew I'd never sit down to study it on my own initiative. However, if I had committed to developing and presenting a two-hour training, I would become something of an expert in the process, wouldn't I? Well, this is what I hoped for, at any rate.

It so happened my architecture training was very well received by those in attendance. Furthermore, the staff of the Training section saw the session's immediate applicability to future Appraiser Trainee classes.

The extent of my training class's architecture instruction had been a three-page hand-out showing sketches of general residential styles, basic roof configurations, and several common window types.

The head of the Training section asked me to give the presentation to the next class of trainees. The session went over so well, I was asked to present it annually to each subsequent training class until I left the department for retirement some thirteen years later.

I was taking initiative, and people were noticing. I felt so lucky. The opportunities seemed to present themselves at just the right times, and they were many. I enthusiastically embraced them.

I didn't mind working harder than the average appraiser. It didn't bother me to be "jumping" from assignment to assignment on a never-ending series of learning curves. I was having a great time. I viewed the Assessor's office as a world of variety and opportunity. You just had to be willing to put in a little extra effort.

Given all of these little victories, imagine my dismay when the name of one of my training classmates appeared on a list of appraisers being transferred to the Assessor's highly requested Major Properties division. This particular classmate,

Joanne, was a smart and attractive young woman who had graduated from our training class near the middle of the pack. She had demonstrated not one iota of *extra* initiative since we had joined the department.

Still naïve as to the intricate workings of the office, I wasn't sure what to make of this little "speed bump" on my road to second-career success. I spoke to my Supervising Appraiser about it. She was encouraging, saying I would certainly get my chance.

Then I mentioned Joanne's good fortune to the Chief Appraiser in charge of our entire district office. He said Major Properties had been asking for motivated people like me. But he'd told them too many of our district's appraisers had been transferred out in the past few months and demanded they look elsewhere this time around. He also told me he was a great believer in making promotion and transfer decisions *according to seniority.*

Seniority! Oh no. Here I was in my mid-40s, with an entire engineering career behind me, and I was going to have to *wait my turn?!* Would all that extra initiative be for naught? Had my classmate Joanne simply been in the right place at the right time, working under a Chief Appraiser who cared little about how many appraisers had recently been snatched from his realm by other regions or divisions? Had she been lucky enough to be assigned to a Chief whose personal philosophy put far less stock in seniority, and far more in potential and promise?

I realized this may well have been the case. I panicked.

I went back to my supervisor and begged her to help me find a way out of our district office. Mind you, this office was more than conveniently located about twelve blocks from my home. But if this Chief intended to prevent me from taking a faster-than-average route to my career goals in spite of all of my extra effort, I wanted to work for another Chief.

Again serendipity intervened, this time under the guise of a "special project" at the main office. When my supervisor was queried by a group leader downtown as to whom she might recommend to assist on the high-profile project, she recommended *me*. This was the opportunity I was looking for – a stint at our headquarters downtown.

Since the group leader didn't know me, he originally committed to a two-week trial, affording himself the option to send me back if I didn't work out. I never returned to that district office. Well, I did, but years later and under very desirable circumstances. But that's another story.

The special project did, in fact, turn out to be very high profile, an aspect whose benefits I'd scarcely considered when I first came on board. The project had to do with the creation of a new computer program for tracking certain details of our work.

I thoroughly enjoyed participating in decision making with the Information Technology staff who were developing the program. I contributed formatting and content ideas, and eventually became a crucial part of the troubleshooting of glitches and other issues. I also wrote the program's on-line user guides – a chance for me to employ my creative talents. When staff began using the program, I was the one they emailed with problems they found.

For months I set up training sessions, in which I had a fabulous time instructing most of the department's fourteen hundred employees on the use of the program. I even set up one-on-one sessions with each upper manager, including the gauntlet throwing master of intimidation from my first day of training.

The group leader who had taken me on became a good friend. I would accompany him and his cronies to lunch most days. I was having the time of my life!

I stayed on the project eight months, leaving only for an opportunity to appraise major commercial properties, as I was convinced the move would get me promoted faster.

The group leader and friend, who wanted me to work with him on his next project, reluctantly let me go. I was sorry to leave Special Projects, which had without a doubt proven the most fun I'd ever had on any job. But I was excited at the prospect of yet another opportunity, this time in the assessor's Major Properties division.

Recall Major Properties was the coveted assignment thrown into the lap of my classmate Joanne. When I started there, my cubicle was near hers. We grew a bit closer. She'd been there about a year when I arrived.

As filled with anticipation as I was upon transferring to Major Properties, I didn't exactly get off to a running start. I had been diagnosed with breast cancer a couple of months before, and had spent my last two months on the special project recovering from a lumpectomy – surgery to remove a cancerous tumor in my breast.

Had the surgery removed all of the cancer? Had the cancer spread to the lymph nodes? Fortunately, the news from my doctor was all good. But I still had a few more medical details to contend with.

It turned out, my first day in Major Properties was also my first day of radiation treatments. I would spend the beginning seven weeks of my new assignment going to the hospital each morning before work to have my treatment. At least my doctor wasn't recommending chemotherapy. I was so relieved.

Did the cancer constitute a "speed bump"? Yes, of course, but a very temporary one. Barely a blip on the radar screen, in fact. And it gave me an excuse to take a little breather as I willingly began the ascent of yet another rather steep learning curve.

My new supervisor generously cut me some slack while I was having those treatments. Although I felt fine, I accepted the slack. I needed a break.

After seven weeks of radiation, the skin on my breast was itchy and purple from "radiation sunburn." No pain, just itch.

Little by little the itch went away and the color of the skin on my breast gradually returned to normal. The cancer had been more an inconvenience than an illness. I'd never felt sick, or even fatigued. Just a little scared.

Cancer is a funny thing. It changes your sense of your own mortality. It takes years to shake the feeling you are vulnerable and could possibly die this month or next. The feeling never completely goes away.

With the cancer *physically* behind me, I strove to give my Major Properties assignment my best effort.

Then a cute thing happened...

My boss handed me an order for business cards, as was standard practice whenever an appraiser changed to a new assignment. He also gave me two additional orders, one for himself and another for the Chief of Major Properties, as he and the Chief were both running low on cards. I was to take the three orders up to the assessor's Reprographics section.

When I arrived at Repro, the guys working there knew me and were happy to have me pay them a visit. In my prior Special Projects assignment, I'd trained them some months earlier on the new program we were all now using daily.

I handed them the three business card orders. They said to tell my boss and the Chief they were running about four weeks behind and hoped the delay in filling the order wouldn't be an inconvenience. I passed on the message.

To my surprise, I received a call from Repro about 45 minutes later telling me I could pick up the business cards. I figured they'd had a change of heart, deciding to prioritize our orders, after all.

I returned to Repro and was handed my business cards. Just mine. I asked about the cards for my boss and the Chief and was told they'd have to wait the four weeks.

I smiled and thanked the Repro staff, resisting the urge to laugh out loud.

I realized the Repro guys knew nothing of appraisal staff hierarchy. They just liked me, knew I'd been the one to give them their training, and assumed I was someone important.

I'd already assessed my new boss to be a man with a decent sense of humor. So, I told him the story. He thought it was very funny and charitably stated he was glad I already had my new business cards. He said he and the Chief would be more than happy to wait their turn.

Life was fairly uneventful for a few months until it was finally rumored promotions would soon be announced. The promotional exam for Appraiser Specialist – the next position up from Appraiser, and my ultimate goal of goals since joining the department – had been given a few months earlier.

With so little experience behind us, my classmates and I passed the exam with varying results. Joanne and I, and two other classmates, had placed in the "reachable" third band, with our other classmates all placing in "unreachable" lesser bands. No one ever gets into the first band. And a handful of veteran appraisers made the very desirable Band 2.

I didn't worry too much about being promoted. I wasn't in the second band, and I knew, given the probable number of openings, it really wasn't time yet for anyone from my class to become an Appraiser Specialist. There were too many other appraisers who were more deserving.

Still, I couldn't help thinking, with my relatively fast track of accomplishments thus far, and the very high-profile special project I'd just successfully completed, management might just see fit to promote me now. I fantasized about the possibility, knowing if anyone from my class were promoted, it would surely be me.

Then the unthinkable happened. The promotion list came out and I wasn't on it, but my classmate Joanne was. She would be getting the prestige, as well as the hefty $8,500.00 per year increase in pay.

The sickness in the pit of my stomach that afternoon, and for many months afterwards, is a feeling I would not wish even on the cell phone-distracted driver who just cut me off. I was, in a word, devastated – shattered to a degree that surprised even me.

The careless politics of an organization, public sector or private, that would permit someone who hadn't attempted to take any extra initiative whatsoever since joining its ranks to be promoted ahead of someone so much more deserving, was far more than I could accept.

Joanne hadn't gotten the highest grade our trainer had ever given to a trainee's narrative appraisal; I had. She hadn't graduated at the top of the class; I had earned that glorious distinction. She hadn't created and presented two well-received in-house trainings; I was the one who had produced those successful PowerPoints. She hadn't participated on a high-profile special project in which her supervisor was absolutely thrilled with her work; that too was me.

And rubbing salt into my emotional sores and lesions was the fact Joanne was almost twenty years younger than me. She hadn't brought to the department the knowledge, skill, and experience of a prior career as an engineer.

In truth, the only thing Joanne had accomplished over me was having made it to Major Properties almost a year earlier. Okay, so Joanne had gotten lucky. I would tell this to myself over and over. I would also attempt to salve my wound with the knowledge that, if I had started in Major Properties when Joanne had, I would never have been offered the chance to participate on the special project I'd so thoroughly enjoyed.

Maybe I needed to look at the big picture and know that, in the long run, my career will have meant so much more than Joanne's because of the care and effort I had given it. In the end, I started to see things this way. The survivor would survive.

If there is one thing I've learned and of which I am now certain, it is that all of the adverse events in our lives happen in order to teach us things. As with my bout with breast cancer, having to endure the excruciating pain of Joanne's promotion taught me very valuable lessons about myself and about life.

In fact, if I were given the chance to change history – to be the one promoted and to spare myself the anguish – *I believe I would respectfully decline the offer.*

A year or so later, it was announced the promotional exam for Appraiser Specialist would be given again. Some appraisers who, like me, felt they'd been shafted the last time around, would squander the opportunity in favor of making a statement – a giant "Screw you!" – to management. That's pretty much what happened with my friends Candace and Jim.

Veteran appraiser Candace was still so depressed and angry from her last effort that, despite my persistent attempts to motivate her (including the prospect of celebrating our promotions with a wonderful lunch out – my treat), she was unable to make herself study.

My classmate Jim, on the other hand, was under the misguided assumption no one from the district offices (where he worked) would be promoted no matter what. In a self-destructive and needlessly defeatist frame of mind, he decided not to take the test, but didn't let me know of this ridiculous decision until two days before the exam date – way too late to study sufficiently to make the second band.

Jim's supervisor "forced" him to take the test. Acting as his tough love friend, I didn't mince words. I informed Jim that, in the last go-around, everyone who made Band 2 got promoted no matter where they were assigned. He hadn't realized. Sheesh.

I, on the other hand, the type A, grade A, first-class go-getter, learned just how motivated I could be.

Truth be told, I was almost frozen with fear. I worried the disappointment from Joanne's promotion would make it impossible for me to apply myself to study seriously for the test this time around. After all, Joanne had her promotion and would never have to take this pain-in-the-neck exam ever again. The realization was maddening.

As you might imagine, I was delighted to feel the spark of determination rear up inside my abdomen. Before my studying was finished, the spark had grown into a wildfire, contained within the natural boundaries of my 5'5" frame and threatening to take out everything in its path.

First, I developed a comprehensive study plan for the test, scheduling every spare moment of my time over the two-month period prior to the exam.

Why so much study? Because this particular promotional exam was notorious for covering an impossibly massive amount of material. It included California property tax law, wide ranging departmental policy and systems, and most of present-day appraisal theory.

I even scheduled time at the end of my two-month study calendar to repeat topics I'd studied at the beginning. Lest I forget some of the earlier material, I would revisit it, ensuring I'd be maximally prepared for the test.

This time was my time. I would leave nothing to chance. I would try for Band 1 to ensure I made Band 2. This time they would have no choice other than to promote me.

The exam date came and went. Then I had to put the event out of my mind for many weeks until the results finally became available.

One of the frustrating things about the Appraiser Specialist test is, you're never really sure how you did. And discussing the questions and problems with colleagues only makes matters worse, because many of them confidently espouse erroneous answers and solutions after the fact.

Finally, Personnel mailed out the results. Sam was working just a couple of miles from our house at the time. I'd begged him to go home at lunch hour on the day I thought the letter would arrive in the mail. He called me from home.

"Hi, Sweetie," Sam excitedly greeted me. "The letter came. If I'm reading this chart correctly, it looks like your total score puts you in something called group two."

Band 2! I was as good as promoted. Oh, my gosh. I think I cried at my desk downtown for half an hour.

Of course, before letting poor Sam off the phone so he might get some lunch prior to returning to work, I made him read me every word and every number in the letter to make sure his "group two" interpretation had absolutely been correct. It had been.

The hurt and angst over Joanne's promotion disappeared in the blink of an eye. I had studied my tail off. I had taken the opportunity to learn this material for the third or fourth time since joining the department, with each instance of the learning reinforcing the subject matter within my brain to a greater degree than the time before. Joanne had never learned this stuff so well. She hadn't had to. I was the lucky one, really. *I* was.

Two weeks later, my supervisor was looking for me. Finally, he found me in the hallway and, with a big grin on his face, told me to go immediately up to the office of the once-upon-a-time gauntlet tossing prince of intimidation.

Richard, whom I had actually grown to like very much, and who really wasn't very intimidating at all, was waiting for me in his office with my supervisor's boss, as well as the Chief of Major Properties. He informed me the department was promoting me to Appraiser Specialist, effective a few days hence.

Richard also offered a startling revelation. He told me he'd wanted to include me in the last round of promotions from the prior exam (when Joanne had been promoted), but had been overruled. I had wondered if that could be the case, and was gratified to know I had been his choice all along.

So, what went around came around, or something like that. I was absolutely thrilled to have reached my primary goal in my new career. As lame as it may sound, becoming an Appraiser Specialist, especially in such a short time after joining the department, meant everything to me. I had finally proven to myself I could achieve my own standard of success.

Most important, I had learned such success has far more to do with the process than with the end result.

From this perspective, Joanne is the one who got cheated. You see, she never really had to go through the process.

By the way, Jim got into Band 3 and had a slight chance of promotion before the test was given again. Candace, on the other hand, only made Band 4. She had no chance of promotion from this exam. Regrettably, I don't think upper management heard their protests.

So, as is the case with most of life's heartbreaks, my "saga of sadness" turned out for the best. At least, I insist on seeing it that way.

And having reached my main goal in my new career, I felt strangely in need…

In need of renewed purpose. But this time I was "free" to look both inside and outside my career for my next challenge.

I began eyeing an assignment as field trainer for a class of appraiser trainees, followed by a promotion to Supervising Appraiser. I also fancied myself an author. In due time, I managed to achieve all three.

Part III
Manifestations

Chapter Eight
Lessons Learned from an Intellectually "Impaired" Pet

Cats know more than we think and think more than we know.
– H. P. Lovecraft

At its worst, my type A "toxicity" had me expecting coworkers and others to match my skills and aptitudes head-to-head. Not only were my expectations out of line, but I failed to recognize the valuable attributes these others possessed. Often, they were qualities I lacked.

Long after my cat Spike died, I realized he'd been the perfect metaphor to encapsulate an important lesson I needed to learn. Spike may have possessed a deficiency in an area I considered important. But he more than made up for it in other ways.

Many years ago, I decided on an impulse to find a female kitten suited to the name "Spike." Most of us succumb from time to time to nonsensical whims, and this was one of many to which I would lay claim.

At the time, animal shelters weren't exactly on my radar. Instead, I found a local pet store to begin my search for Spike.

I had scarcely entered the pet shop's door, and there at my feet was a small cage with the most gorgeous little sandy blonde long-haired kitten. It must have been all of six or eight weeks old. Its precious tail was an almost perfect equilateral triangle of fur.

I paused for only a few moments staring at the rather calm and contented little thing.

Already satisfied I had found the ideal pet, I whispered to myself, "That's Spike."

"How much?" I queried the proprietor.

"Oh, ten dollars, I guess," he replied. "It's only been here about fifteen minutes. Someone just dropped it off."

"I'll take her," I stated in a self-assured tone while suppressing my rapidly growing excitement.

Spike would be my first real pet.

I took the kitten home and introduced her to my boyfriend Harry.

"Isn't she *beautiful*?" I proudly exclaimed.

Harry agreed she was indeed stunning. But in looking her over, he wasted no time revealing his findings – Spike was no female.

"Check out the size of these paws… among other things," Harry advised, exhibiting a surprising level of expertise on the subject. "This is a male cat and he's gonna be *big*."

It was a reasonable mistake for me to have made, considering what a beauty Spike was. For years afterwards, even veterinarians would take one look at Spike and refer to him as "she." In spite of his name and size, he was far too pretty to be a male cat, and everyone just assumed he was a girl.

Okay, so Spike was a boy. No problem. After all, if I'd cared very much about the sex of the animal, I would have done a little "research" before adopting.

Spike grew to be the extra-large specimen Harry had predicted. And he really was too beautiful for words. He had a thick white undercoat and a champagne long-haired top coat with faint tabby-striped markings.

His face was perfectly symmetrical with big green eyes. His tail, a marvel of feline engineering, extended over a foot long, was almost perfectly cylindrical, and made such a fluffy presentation it probably measured two-and-a-half inches in diameter.

Spike turned out to be a great cat. For me, at least, he was perfect. I wanted a pet willing to sit on my lap for hours at a time, and that was exactly the kitty I got. Purring away, Spike sat and sat and sat and sat.

Spike was also what I would call a "bed cat." This evocative term came from an amusing pretend advertisement I once heard on a weekly radio show. There was a (fictitious) special that week on "bed cats" – enormous fuzzy cats. The ad promised prospective buyers that a three-by-three matrix of these extra-large "heater cats" would afford maximum coverage of your queen-size bed to help get you through the cold winter nights.

This too described Spike. Of course, I had only one Spike, not a grid of nine. But when he lay down, he seemed to spread out across a wide berth in all directions. And he emitted lots of heat.

The only thing "wrong" with Spike was, well, he was not very bright.

Other cats I've had since Spike have learned simple things fairly quickly. For example, if I decided to move the food bowl from one end of the kitchen to the other, the cat might initially wait for the food at the bowl's usual spot. So, I would pick up the cat and carry it to the relocated bowl. At that point, the cat might check both the old and new locations once or twice before giving up on the prior site altogether.

Not Spike. It could take weeks of transporting him across the kitchen each morning before he finally caught on.

Understand that taking on Spike was a big move for this type A. Type A's like to be in control, and for every pet acquired at least a little control is given up. What if the animal destroys personal property? What if it gets sick or injured and must be taken to the vet? In either case, think of the potential financial consequences. And there's the responsibility for feeding. Not to mention, the cat must be cared for if I leave town for the weekend, or go on vacation.

So, adopting Spike represented a baby step toward relinquishing some of the tight rein I maintained over my life. I'd guessed my exacting nature had prevented me from experiencing life to the fullest. This was my way of letting go, just a little.

Spike also taught me something about sentient beings of less than formidable intelligence: *What they lack in smarts they might just offset in other ways.*

The revelation should have been an early lesson to counter my unreasonable expectations of others. But at the time, I wasn't paying close enough attention to absorb the implications of such a fitting analogy. So, I'll make use of the example now, many years later.

This is the tale of the three most impressive things Spike ever did.

Spike's first "shocker" may suggest greater intelligence than I ever gave him credit for. I guess you'll have to decide for yourself.

In my late 20s, not long after adopting Spike, I rented a fabulous apartment in a wonderful historic building near Griffith Park in L.A. There were fourteen apartments in the complex, with no two alike. Being a lover of significant architecture, I was in my element.

Spike and I settled into our new home together, and everything fell into place. I loved the neighborhood and became acquainted with the couple who lived across the courtyard. Spike went in and out as he pleased. He even befriended a skunk! Yep, but that's a story for another day.

After living there for a couple of years, I was making a sudden job change and wanted to grab the opportunity to take a three-week trip to England, Scotland and Wales. My friends across the courtyard offered to look after Spike while I was away.

When I returned, Spike looked healthy and well cared for. I thanked my neighbors for their generous willingness to see to his needs during my travels.

I commenced unpacking my suitcase in the bedroom. The task completed, I headed into the living room where I was surprised to glimpse Spike crouching on the fireplace mantle. He'd never jumped up there before.

On the mantle I'd placed a carefully arranged set of figurines depicting an orchestra, complete with a conductor and an opera singer. On closer examination, I realized Spike was quite intentionally positioned there with his paw poised right behind the opera singer. He'd clearly been waiting there for me to enter the room and look in his direction.

Like a golfer teeing off, Spike swiped the opera singer off the mantle!

As I gasped in horror, he jumped down onto the floor and darted away, perhaps hiding under the bed until I cooled my jets.

It only took a few moments for me to realize Spike had expressed his displeasure over my leaving him for three weeks. His appalling act of defiance was simply his way of communicating his profound dissatisfaction. I think he was also warning me never to do that to him again.

Honestly, I was impressed. I didn't know Spike had it in him.

Spike's next feat, and arguably his most impressive…

My first marriage was a mismatch of notable proportion. (You'll read all about it in Chapter 9.) What's relevant for purposes of relating Spike's second stunning performance is that my husband Darren came to our new married life with a cat. Her name was Doofy, and believe me, I could write a chapter alone on her.

Darren had found Doofy on the streets of New York City. In sharp contrast to Spike, Doofy was, without a doubt, the homeliest cat I'd ever seen. She was skinny and white with black ears and three huge black spots on her back. One ear had a chunk missing, the result of some cat fight or night of "rough love." In addition, each of Doofy's paws had not five, not six, but *seven* claws. She was so narrow, and her paws so wide, her extra toes came just short of tripping over one another as she walked.

Poor Doofy? I don't think so. Doofy carried herself with such an upright and regal presence, you'd think she were the Queen of Sheba. She seemed to believe she was the most exquisite cat on the planet.

Doofy was also smart as a whip. When Darren moved in with Doofy, guess who ruled the roost? I'll give you a hint. It wasn't my Spike, who was almost three times Doofy's size.

On the first day, a peevish Doofy, probably anticipating a territorial power struggle, appeared uncomfortable in her new home. In a naïve gesture of what appeared to be friendship, Spike ran up to greet his new housemate. Not a wise move. Doofy took a claw swipe at Spike's nose, drawing a little blood.

Spike remained at least somewhat intimidated by her for the duration of their years in the same home.

The four of us – Darren and I and the two kitties – established our life together, such as it was. Spike and Doofy seemed to cohabitate peacefully by keeping their distance from one another, as far as we could tell.

A few months later, we moved our household to another part of the city. We kept the cats inside for the recommended couple of weeks to allow them to acclimate to their new surroundings. When we finally let them outside our apartment, the man living downstairs warned us there was a feral cat hanging around and antagonizing the neighborhood cats.

But what could we do? Our cats weren't accustomed to being indoors all the time. They liked to come and go. We felt we had no choice but to take our chances with the troublemaking wild cat.

A few days later, the same neighbor hurriedly approached me when I arrived home from work. He told me there had been a terrible cat fight, which had begun with the feral cat attacking my "black and white cat." He said my "big fluffy beige cat" soon came to the rescue to finish off the feral feline offender.

He said he'd looked around for both of my cats after the incident, but couldn't find them. He also reported the feral cat had limped away bleeding and looking like it might not make it. He led me to where I could see the feral cat's blood on the sidewalk.

I walked around the property calling Spike's and Doofy's names. Doofy was nowhere to be found, and I was concerned.

But Spike soon came trotting over. I inspected him closely. There wasn't a scratch on him!

I asked the neighbor if he was certain it had been Spike who had defeated the feline bully. He told me there was no doubt whatsoever it had been Spike.

It appeared my lap/bed cat, who had never previously been known to harbor a hostile intention of any kind, possessed the instincts of a Samurai. It made a sort of sense. A blind person develops other senses more fully. The intelligence-challenged Spike had simply been blessed with another kind of "intelligence."

Sometime later that evening we found Doofy under a bush, her face scratched up and swollen to twice its size. She looked madder than hell. We wanted to have our vet check her out, but the look in her eyes told us she needed to cool off first. We let her be.

The next morning, Doofy showed up at the back door of the apartment. The swelling in her face had reduced substantially. We decided not to take her to the vet unless further problems arose. She turned out to be fine, healing up fully in just a couple of days.

We wondered if Spike and Doofy would become closer as a result of their harrowing experience. It wasn't to be. Things returned to the way they had been, with the peace-loving Spike having attained the rank of dominant cat in the neighborhood, if not in our household.

Spike and Doofy continued to maintain their distance from one another, but for an inexplicable thing that happened one day.

I made an uncharacteristic lunch hour stop at home. When I pulled up in front of our apartment building, Spike and Doofy were sitting side-by-side on the front apartment's stoop. Darren and I had never seen our two cats this close in proximity. Not since their initial meeting when Doofy let Spike know who would be boss.

I was incredulous. What could this mean?

When I got out of the car, the cats saw me and immediately dispersed like arrows shot from two crossbows pointed in opposite directions. The phenomenon of their voluntary alliance on the stoop that day remains a mystery.

Spike's third surprise…

One morning a couple of years later, we opened the back door to let the cats in, as we did every morning. The always ravenous Spike was there, but Doofy was strangely absent. We coaxed Spike to have some breakfast.

For the first time ever, he wasn't interested in food. He kept running halfway down the rear stairs and back up again.

Having forgotten about Spike's rather impressive opera singer incident from several years prior, I said to Darren, "This may sound ridiculous, because we know Spike is utterly incapable of complex reasoning. But it looks like he wants us to follow him."

We did, and Spike led us to the place on the side walkway where Doofy lay dead. Flies buzzed about her foamy mouth. There was no sign she'd been attacked, but likely died of some sort of natural cardiac arrest.

I cried my eyes out.

Having done his "brotherly" duty, Spike went up to have his breakfast. And that morning I'm pretty sure he didn't eat nearly as much as usual.

Chapter Nine
Scenes from a Marriage

Happily ever after is not a fairy tale, it's a choice.
— Fawn Weaver

As you now know, I found a near-perfect match in my husband Sam. He was the divinely inspired companion of my fondest dreams, and he was my *second* spouse. Darren had been my first. And to say the five-year ordeal we endured together was a rough ride is to understate the situation considerably.

Darren and I were both type A, which is not necessarily a deal-breaker. But we were emotionally undisciplined, a fact that yielded abundant sparks on a good day. On a bad one, a raging wildfire pales in comparison.

My five-year "speed bump" of a marriage to Darren may have robbed me of some of the best years of my life, but it also forced a "hard turn" onto a "switchback" leading to bigger and better things.

Do any of the mistakes we make amount to time *wasted?* I don't think so.

Turning thirty was a tough birthday for me. In fact, it was the only one I found hard to reconcile.

Feeling fine that day I nevertheless called in sick to work, something that would never happen under normal circumstances.

I took the phone off the hook. (Today one would "silence" one's "cell.") I stood in front of the mirror for at least 45 minutes inspecting my face for wrinkles. I didn't shower or even get dressed. I just waited for the sorry day to end. The following day, I was back to my usual self.

What was *that* all about?

Honestly, I'm not sure. But I can offer a possibility.

For me, my thirtieth birthday must have represented a deadline of sorts. Suddenly time was up. I'd better find someone to marry within the next year or two, or having children would be out of the question. Even if I found Mr. Right during the two-year time frame I'd arbitrarily given myself, the wedding likely wouldn't take place until at least a year later, and more realistically, two years. The clock was ticking…

Darren and I met through mutual acquaintances while in engineering school at UCLA. He was a large man, 6'2" tall, with blonde hair and an outgoing personality. I appreciated Darren's intelligent conversation, futuristic dreams and ideas, and excitement for life. I liked his friends and his cat.

After we'd been together for a year-and-a-half or so, Darren must have proposed. Oddly, I don't recall the event.

Having agreed to get married, I was thrilled to finally be planning my wedding. But I never stopped to wonder if we were doing the right thing. Had I found the right man? Had he found his soulmate in me? What would a lifelong commitment to Darren look like?

It must have been self-evident I should give the marriage more thought. But I'm sure I felt backed into a corner, believing… if I didn't marry now, the chance to fulfill the only vision I'd ever had for a happy family life with a loving husband and kids might evaporate for good. It amounted to a "hail Mary" uncharacteristic of my usual meticulous *modus operandi*.

I pressed on, conscientiously arranging for the big day.

Then, the week leading up to the wedding, the unimaginable happened. Darren lost his engineering job.

My parents did not mince words. They hadn't been in favor of the marriage from the start, as they saw Darren as headstrong and brash. Now he might depend on their daughter for his livelihood. The prospect didn't sit well with Mom and Dad. Not well at all.

But I knew Darren would not want to sit idle. He loved being an aerospace engineer and would surely seek reemployment as soon as possible.

Darren and I said our vows at the wedding we'd both wanted, with everyone in attendance. It was very exciting.

And here is a secret I've kept until now...

> *As we said our vows, I had an overwhelming urge to flee. Obviously, the much-needed clarity I received was extremely ill-timed. I simply couldn't bring myself to stop the proceedings as they were happening. Others have done so, leaving their betrothed at the altar. But I couldn't do it. I knew I had to follow through and let the consequences play out.*

After a honeymoon I can scarcely remember, Darren and I settled into married life. He immediately applied for a job in the Airlock Outfitting Group for the new space station project. The problem was, this group would not be forming for another year-and-a-half. And Darren wasn't certain he'd be selected when the time came. But he assured me he was highly confident he'd be offered the job and informed me he had plans to do other things during the interim months.

And he did. Sort of.

Darren registered for some graduate-level engineering courses. He also took a temporary gig with a friend who designed, built and installed high-end audio-visual systems for large corporate clients.

We made ends meet mostly on my salary. But I still felt the pressure of my parents' disapproval of Darren's *under*employment. I desperately wanted to be free of that albatross around my neck.

After the initial few months, in which Darren stayed fairly busy with the classes and side job, those opportunities had played themselves out. He was suddenly lacking for anything to do with himself. He was despondent, and the engineering job opportunity was still at least a year away.

I had noticed a "Help Wanted" sign at the service deli at our local grocery store and asked Darren if he'd like to apply. It seemed like the perfect option. It was close to home, would give him something to do and would bring in some money. I was pretty sure Darren's depressed mood would benefit, as well.

For some reason, Darren viewed my suggestion as unconscionable. He said he would never forgive me.

I was perplexed by his reaction, but couldn't get him to explain it in a meaningful way.

In any case, he did apply at the supermarket, and got the service deli position. After a week or two, it seemed Darren liked the job well enough, and it appeared to be a great temporary solution to our main problem.

But we were arguing all the time. The combination of my anxiety level over my parents' disapproval of our situation, and Darren's resentment over my suggesting he apply at the market, was more than our new marriage could easily bear.

Darren was distant. Apparently, he really did intend to hold a grudge against me for the foreseeable future. And he refused to talk about it.

I was utterly miserable. I felt trapped in a marriage to a man who would barely speak to me. And I wasn't certain I'd ever really loved Darren to begin with.

But I'd made a commitment. And I intended to do my best to see it through. I guess you could say I'd made a decision to stay put while suffering in silence. And for the time being, that's what I did.

I made the best of things by concentrating on my job, playing in a community orchestra I'd joined and seeing friends. Life could have been much worse.

Many months later, I arrived home from work one day to find a buoyant Darren. He was excited and smiling. He had finally received a call from the team leader of the space station project's Airlock Outfitting Group. Darren had been offered the staff engineering position, which would start in two weeks.

We were ecstatic.

Darren had the aerospace job he'd coveted, and for which we'd waited almost two years! And I finally had a husband with full-time work that would garner my parents' approval.

It instantly seemed things might work out, after all, for Darren and me.

We decided to move across town, where we'd both be closer to our jobs. After a year or so, we even bought a house. (I stayed in that house for 24 years!)

Pretty soon Darren and a co-worker started a community "space society." They would hold meetings with interesting speakers. Even our local congressman found out about it and joined. I helped out with refreshments.

The space club made things a little better for a while. It felt like Darren and I had a common goal, something we could do together. Darren seemed self-assured and happy.

One day I arrived home from work and pushed the button on our answering machine. As I changed out of my work clothes while listening to the play-back, one of the messages stopped me cold.

"Hello, this message is for Darren. This is Buzz Aldrin. Darren, do you still need a speaker for your meeting next Tuesday night? I think I can be available. Please call me back at (xxx) xxx-xxxx."

Darren arrived home a short time later. I played Buzz Aldrin's message for him. He seemed to take it in stride as if it were not a big deal!

At any rate, exciting things were happening.

But we were still arguing all the time, about seemingly everything. I viewed Darren as unreasonable. Having a constructive conversation with him was nearly impossible. And he seemed to derive satisfaction from "pushing me around." Our relationship was out of control.

I didn't want to be the one to break us up. So, I continued on as best I could, enduring what was increasingly an intolerable marriage.

Until one day when, out of the blue, Darren announced, "Vic, it's time we had children."

In disbelief I replied, "Darren, this marriage is nowhere near solid enough for children."

"But I want kids," he repeated.

I finally saw my way out.

After carefully collecting my thoughts, I responded, "Then we should divorce so you can find someone with whom having children makes sense."

The color drained from Darren's face. And for the first time it dawned on me, he didn't view our marriage the way I did. He seemed to think it was perfectly fine.

Darren pleaded, "But I love you."

Perhaps insensitively I replied, "I don't really think you do."

And that was it. We divorced.

And even our divorce was plagued by "speed bumps," everything from Darren draining our bank account to him totaling his car. He even delayed the divorce's finalization by making unnecessary special requests of the attorney.

But the day eventually came when the divorce was final. And my five-year nightmare, made all the more unbearable by my type A chaos-aversion, ended. I'd seldom felt so relieved and at peace.

Chapter Ten
Ollalieberry (sp?) Madness

If my holding out those berries was an act of temporary insanity, then those people will embrace insanity too.
— Suzanne Collins

The type A personality, for all of its commonly known attributes, exhibits some nuanced traits not often discussed. One such characteristic is what I will call "mission susceptibility."

Have you ever known a person who suddenly makes it her goal to accomplish something trivial as if it were of the utmost importance? And she takes on this obsession for no other reason than... well, just because?

I guess the perpetually keyed-up type A has to find a way to get some fun out of life. And what better way to do it than to indulge the only way she knows how – type A nonsense.

One evening many years ago my childhood friend Aaron, my soon-to-be-husband Sam, and I embarked on a mission – to find the quintessential fresh ollalieberry (sp?) pie.

At the time, I lived in a lovely section of Long Beach, California, where finding several examples of this rare and highly sought after treat was a piece o' cake. (Pun intended.) In those days one could find four versions of this June-only sensation within a single square mile.

So, why would we – a high-priced attorney, a travel professional and an engineer – make pie an evening's obsession? Why not?

You see, Aaron and I always loved a good contest. My sweet Sam honestly couldn't have cared less which restaurant's pie was the best. He just came along for the ride, his earnest hope... to eventually sit down and enjoy a slice.

Anyway, it all began the prior July when, in the normal course of conversation, Aaron and I happened upon the very important matter of how the ollalieberry (sp?) came into being. With ample authority, Aaron proclaimed the ollalieberry (sp?) to be a cross between a loganberry and a marionberry.

I spoke up without hesitation, "Oh no, Aaron, I'm quite certain the ollalieberry (sp?) is a cross between a loganberry and a *youngberry*."

"A youngberry!" Aaron bellowed. "What's that?!"

"I don't know," I answered a bit defensively. "Some kind of blackberry. Polly's menu used to describe it exactly that way – 'a cross between a loganberry and a youngberry.' I read it so many times, I could never forget it."

Aaron refused to yield, an unfortunate commentary on either my memory or Polly's' credibility... or both.

Before we knew it, Aaron and I had shaken hands cementing another in a long line of friendly but (make no mistake) serious bets – a unifying staple of our then 25-year friendship. The loser was to buy the winner an ollalieberry (sp?) pie the following June.

With the terms of the wager well defined, we set out to obtain proof of the ollalieberry's (sp?) true parentage.

Having contacted a variety of expert sources, jurisdictions and pie shops, I was perplexed to find the collected responses were anything but conclusive. One young man at Russell's, a local Long Beach diner, insisted the ollalieberry (sp?) resulted from the coupling of a marionberry and a boysenberry. (Hmph. What did he know?)

Polly's, though apparently no longer willing to commit it to print, maintained that responsibility for our ever-popular little berry indeed lies with the loganberry and the youngberry. Jongevaard's Bake & Broil concurred, as did Hof's Hut (sort of).

The Chamber of Commerce of the California town of Cambria, yet another ollalieberry (sp?) hot spot, wasn't quite certain whether the loganberry was paired with an Oregon blackberry or a youngberry. I said it must assuredly be the youngberry. They agreed.

Finally, Sam partially saved the day when he produced a book he just happened to have at his condominium – a fruit book with a chapter on berries. It regrettably did not specify the origin of the ollalieberry (sp?). But... it did state the marionberry was derived *from* the ollalieberry (sp?) and some other berry. Ah-hah!

Although the ollalieberry (sp?) seems to take great joy in depriving us of the satisfaction of absolute certainty, it nevertheless appears our "friend" is indeed a cross between a loganberry and a youngberry. I presented my findings to Aaron. He conceded. (What a sport.)

So, this is how the three of us came to spend a Tuesday evening the following June making the rounds of four well-known Long Beach pie establishments in rapid succession. This would be the night we would determine the crème de la crème of fresh (not baked) ollalieberry (sp?) pie. It was Aaron's idea to make a competition out of it. He always took things to extremes.

Moving right along...

Acknowledging we were getting off to a late start, and that Russell's and "the Bake" both close around 9 p.m., we prudently chose to visit them first, even though doing so would result in a bit of zigzagging through the neighborhood. Before leaving the house, I flipped the switch on the coffee maker so we would have fresh hot coffee all ready when we returned home with the "fruits" of our labor.

We arrived at Russell's, and clearly visible through the glass of the display case sat one lone gorgeous pie chock full of huge ollalieberries (sp?). We contemplated purchasing a single slice of the luscious confection. But we realized the pie would surely fall apart if we'd had the restaurant staff cut into it, which would be such a shame. So, Aaron sensibly decided to buy the whole pie. That's the spirit! We were off and running.

Next stop – "the Bake."

"Oh no, it's too far off course, at least seven blocks!" I cried.

So it was that we gave up on our circuitous route designed to ensure we made it to each restaurant before closing. Having thrown caution to the wind, we sped over to Hof's Hut. They have those *little* pies, just the right size so each of us could have two or three tastes. We and our little pie escaped from Hof's in minutes, with plenty of time to get to "the Bake."

Hey, this was easy, literally as easy as pie!

We were energized. We flew into "the Bake" feeling like a trio of superheroes.

"One slice of ollalieberry (sp?) pie to go, please," I ordered, secure in the knowledge nothing could stop us now.

"Oh, I'm sorry, we're all out. It's almost closing time," the girl advised us.

We were dumbstruck.

My type B Sam clearly didn't understand, much less share, the urgency with which Aaron and I pursued our goal.

Sam patted my shoulder with his hand, while saying in a reassuring tone, "It's all right, Sweetie, we already have plenty of ollalieberry (sp?) pie to enjoy."

I gazed up at Aaron, his smile atop the 6'2" stature having soured considerably.

He bleakly moaned, "What do you want to do?"

I turned to the girl behind the counter and, knowing Sam would disapprove, pleaded anyway, "You see, this slice of pie is very important. We're on a mission that cannot entirely succeed if we don't have ollalieberry (sp?) pie from your restaurant... tonight! And this is going to be a story we can tell our grandchildren someday. Isn't there *something* you can do?"

The girl turned to the manager, who stood nearby going through the evening's receipts. He had overheard our dilemma.

Without looking up from his task, he nodded his approval to the young employee, and instructed her, "Go ahead and make one."

Yes! Thank you, thank you, *thank you!* Needless to say, we exited "the Bake" a few minutes later with a *whole pie*.

Now imagine the *1812 Overture* playing over all of Long Beach as we hightailed it to Polly's, the last stop on our now precarious journey. Would Polly's have pie? They're open till 11. No problem.

We pulled up to Polly's and confidently made our way to the counter where a cheerful young girl and guy stood waiting to assist us.

Guess what? No ollalieberry (sp?) pie. Polly's was out.

I looked over at Sam wondering if he'd break our engagement if I pulled the "Bake" routine again at Polly's. But he appeared strangely serene, as though he'd finally succumbed to the mania. Or maybe he figured he'd be eating pie sooner if he didn't rock the boat.

In any case, I couldn't help myself. I went through it again, this time embellishing the story with the suggestion it might appear as a feature in the local paper. But the girl and guy behind the counter, though clearly sympathetic to our plight, remained steadfast, for they had run out of pie glaze.

Feeling almost beaten, we thanked them and contemplated driving to the Polly's at the traffic circle, a few miles away. Then suddenly destiny intervened.

The young man's face lit up. He urged us to wait. He vanished to the back room while we stood by the counter hoping against hope.

Had he joined our cause, jumped on our bandwagon? Evidently he had, for he reappeared minutes later with a genuine Polly's ollalieberry (sp?) pie, complete with glaze. Success! (Insert UCLA fight song here.)

We drove back to the house victorious. The smell of coffee filled the air. We divvied up the pies and discussed the merits of each.

Russell's' had the biggest berries and the most of them, and tasted a lot like boysenberry pie (curious). Polly's' was scrumptious, though a bit heavy on the glaze (even more curious).

"The Bake's" had excellent balance of tartness and sweetness, as did Hof's'. Frankly, they were all delicious, and each of us had a different favorite – honest. So, if you stayed with me hoping for a verdict, I'm sorry to disappoint.

Of course, we only made it through about a fifth of the quantity of pie we'd purchased. Our office mates benefited handsomely the next day.

Last but not least? That would be the issue of the spelling of our frustrating little berry's name.

First, believe me when I say I am one of the world's most consummate spellers. I have a photographic memory for spelling. If I've ever seen a word spelled, I don't forget how to spell it. Furthermore, correct spelling is very important to me. I bristle upon seeing a word misspelled.

With this in mind, I challenge anyone interested to research the spelling of the word "ollalieberry" (sp?) and find proof of the correct spelling. Since it's a name, I will not accept the answer that both spellings (the double "l" first or the single "l" first) are correct. Good luck.

I researched the spelling of "ollalieberry" (sp?) and came up with many authoritative responses on both sides. Even the public library had two differing opinions.

"Why doesn't she just check Sam's fruit book?" you ask.

She did, and found "ollalieberry" (sp?) twice on the same page. It was spelled both ways!

As you might have guessed, I have a love/hate relationship with the ollalieberry (sp?). I love to eat them. And I hate trying to find out anything about them. It's impossible. As for the spelling...

Until such time as I have proof, I have resolved to spell the name the way I personally prefer to spell it (note my consistency throughout this chapter), adding the "(sp?)" to acknowledge I haven't a clue how it is truly supposed to be spelled, and thereby exempting me on this occasion from misspelling a word for the first time in my life.

This is ollalieberry (sp?) madness.

UPDATE: Spellcheck now favors the spelling "olallieberry." This development need not detract from the story told, and I stand by every word. – *VPG*

Chapter Eleven
Road Rage 101

Nothing can be more useful to a man than the determination not to be hurried. – Henry David Thoreau

Road rage, for our purposes here, shall not include the act of chasing after an errant driver in order to do him or her bodily harm. People who use guns, or even verbal threats, to frighten or assault the perpetrator of some idiotic motoring maneuver are way out of control, possessing deep-seated psychological problems far exceeding the hotheadedness typical of the type A road rager.

Of course, road rage at its worst certainly encompasses such behavior. But for this discussion, let's define the phenomenon another way.

Try to imagine an individual who is comfortable behind the wheel only when she is intent upon getting from point A to point B in the least possible amount of time. To the driver in this frame of mind, anything presenting an obstacle to her goal is a "speed bump," whether literal or figurative.

As long as the type A driver can get from point A to point B without anyone or anything getting in the way, things are hunky dory. Granted, she is probably travelling well above the posted speed limit, but her anger and frustration remain in check. All is right with the world.

What are the chances of taking a car anywhere these days without encountering some minor irritation? They are nil. Therefore, the type A driver almost never gets to her destination without something or someone having pissed her off.

I will refrain from too specifically analyzing the motivations behind road rage (even our modified definition), for I am not a psychologist. Still, I feel compelled to relate some of my experience. After all, road rage (per the above modified definition) took over my driving mentality long ago. And although it may well be true that not all type A's suffer from this revolting malady, I feel quite safe in stating that those who road rage are all type A.

Actual speed bumps are the most rudimentary foe of those who road rage (per the above definition, remember). Okay, so now we are talking about literal speed bumps, and not the figurative kind featured prominently in other chapters of this book. I challenge any reader to find me a type A who doesn't loathe those hateful mounds of asphalt intended to cramp our style, annoy us beyond words, slow... us... down.

As if it were all about us. Honestly! But it's true, the generally-on-edge type A sees a speed bump as a personal affront. She doesn't care that the tiny knoll of annoyance was placed there to preserve the safety of school children, shoppers in parking lots, the elderly and the public at large. She is only willing to acknowledge the inconvenience of the horrid thing.

Several years ago, it seemed all of the children on our street were under ten years of age. Many of the parents, being understandably hypersensitive to "speeding" cars on a street where their children were skateboarding and playing baseball, began a campaign to have speed bumps installed on our little residential "thoroughfare."

The City approval apparently required the signatures of every single homeowner on our two-block-long street. Imagine my horror when I was asked to sign the petition requesting the city allow, on our street, the installation of speed bumps – one of the top ten from my personal list of primary life aggravations.

I understood the parents' concerns. But did they have any idea what they were asking of me? I thought about what it would be like to leave home and return, in each case having to slow down to a crawl, subject my body to the inherent jarring, then move on to the next bump where I would be compelled to go through the same unpleasantness yet again.

I apologized, saying I would respectfully decline signing the petition. Apparently (gulp) I was the only one who refused to sign. Eventually the neighbors got over their disgust, their kids having all made it to adulthood. Most of them resumed treating me with friendship and goodwill.

Getting back to the figurative "speed bump," it dots the landscape of highways and byways within virtually all modern-day urban environments. It makes its unwelcome appearance in the form of late-night road construction, various traffic accidents, miscellaneous lane closures, as well as the usual stop-and-go congestion choking the freeways due to desperately needed upgrades to city infrastructure.

On further breakdown, we might also include stalled vehicles, furniture and other large debris in lanes, and the most insidious of all heels-on-wheels – the vigilante driver. This passive-aggressive human irritant drives 55 MPH in the fast lane. He also lines up with other vigilantes across three or more lanes forming a 55 MPH "wall of traffic" that no other driver, no matter how skilled or motivated, can get around. As long as there are road ragers, the vigilante driver is essentially a dim-wit with a death wish.

A primary frustration of she who road rages is another road rager.

"How dare he cut me off!"

Never mind the fact that he did exactly what she just did to some other poor sap. Road ragers have no tolerance for other road ragers. The illogic required of those who road rage defies all explanation.

I can personally attest to having felt more fury negotiating the freeways of Southern California than in any other aspect of life. Nothing else comes close.

In an effort, I think, to shame myself into curtailing my road rage, I have sometimes admitted to others that I absolutely detest other drivers. I'm sure this sounds outlandish to them, as I am overall a very nice, well-behaved woman (believe it or not). But the sentiment is heartfelt, however extreme it may sound.

This is the dilemma of the good citizen, type A road rager. Our road rage doesn't fit our otherwise responsible and well-mannered demeanor.

For what it's worth, I adhere to a self-devised arbitrary rule disallowing the screaming of obscenities and the flipping off of others. I believe bad language and nasty gestures are trashy.

And I cannot abide lowering myself to trashiness. Therefore, I always find another way to express my motoring displeasure.

As if my road rage didn't lack class by virtue of its very existence. Still, I feel I must make certain refinements where possible. Just more evidence nothing about road rage makes much sense.

Here's something worthy of mention... A road rager doesn't *always* road rage. Certain distractions seem to preempt the behavior. If a favorite song is playing on the radio, and I feel inclined to sing my little heart out, my driving "consciousness" transforms into some sort of instinctive auto-pilot. The same thing happens when I sink deep into thought about some recent event, or when I mentally leave the real world to dream up an imaginary conversation to deal with an upsetting recent circumstance.

When I finally emerge from this trance-like state, I may well have gone a few miles beyond my destination. More to the point, I am amazed at the state of my driving. My velocity is exactly the ambient speed of traffic in my lane. I am a good conservative distance from the car ahead of me. I have made no one angry. On dazed auto-pilot, my driving becomes the very example of courtesy, skill and patience.

We can conclude, then, road rage requires the full attention and concentration of the road rager. What a colossal waste of time and mental energy.

There is one other instance in which I will not road rage. On the relatively rare occasion in which I have one or more passengers in my car, I feel wholly responsible for their well-being. I genuinely feel I have no right to subject them to the hostility, ugliness and increased danger resulting from my road rage. (Unfortunately, Sam was sometimes an exception to this rule.)

Or perhaps I'm kidding myself. Maybe the truth is, I didn't want friends and family (other than Sam, apparently) to witness this shameful aspect of my defective character. After all, road rage appears to flourish in part because of the anonymity drivers perceive they have when they are confined alone within their automobiles. Still, I would like to believe the former is true in my case.

At the risk of stating the obvious, patience is not the strong suit of the type A. Road rage is all about impatience. Furthermore, it becomes so habitual, it rears up even in those extraordinary instances in which the type A is not in any particular hurry.

It's true. Having finished all my week's errands, and with the house in order, cars washed, dishes and laundry done, saved articles read, and recorded television programs all watched, I might breathe a very self-satisfied sigh of relief and wonder what the heck to do now.

You see, the type A's main goal in life is to be absolutely caught up with all obligations. But on the rare occasion this state of affairs actually exists, the type A is uncomfortably out of her element.

No matter. She decides to go for a walk at a nearby nature reserve. But no sooner has she positioned herself behind the wheel of her car than the great menacing monster begins to emerge. She is already driving faster than necessary. She honks at the driver in front of her who let pass a perfectly good opportunity to make his turn.

When she arrives at her destination, she approaches a parking space to find that the car parked next to it is carelessly positioned well over the line rendering her space too small. She curses the moron who parked it.

By the time she begins her Sunday afternoon walk, she is her usual hostile wrought-up type A self. She even walks more briskly than she has to. Can she just relax?! Believe me, it ain't easy.

Like most cultural extremes, road rage may well be self-limiting. If this unseemly vice has progressed to the point at which road ragers themselves have become intimidated by other road ragers, their fear may well outweigh the propensity to road rage. We can only hope.

For my part, I have noted a distinct cowardice in myself when feeling obliged to react with an admonishing stare or "inquiry" to the misdeed of another driver. These days I generally look over to ascertain whom I am dealing with before I fix my sternly judgmental gaze upon the jerk. If the object of my scorn is a young guy in a fast car, I probably won't mess with him.

It also helps to have a calming influence in one's life. My husband Sam never hesitated to express his condemnation of some of my less constructive type A "eccentricities." My road rage enjoyed top billing for Sam's disapproval. You won't hear any complaints from me. That is, not unless some fool just forced me to slam on my brakes!

When I first began to road rage years ago, I recall being one of very few. It was especially evident almost no women engaged in this unbecoming behavior.

Furthermore, the term "road rage" had yet to be coined.

At that time, the vast majority of drivers were courteous, but I saw them as losers with little skill and no sense of urgency. To me they were merely obstacles to get around.

The freeways were less packed with traffic back then, and news reports of one driver threatening another were unheard of. So, the fledgling road rager was empress of the avenue, queen of the causeway, virtually invincible.

Today the road rager seems more the rule than the exception. But I am happy to report I am no longer a member of their ranks. I have finally managed to undo an almost lifelong bad habit.

These days, while tooling around town in my car, I cruise tranquilly amidst a sea of impatient drivers. Now I am the one being prevented from changing lanes in time to exit the freeway at my desired off-ramp. And I feel a lump form in my throat as it occurs to me, I was one of the aggressive drivers who started this unfortunate trend.

Epilogue

He who has a why to live can bear almost any how.
— Friedrich Nietzsche

Yes, I conquered my road rage. And my impatience has diminished. It was hard work.

Moving to a small town has helped. When the aggravations are fewer and farther between, the intervals separating them afford the "perp" some much needed breathing room.

I would love to claim these reforms are wholly the product of my own initiative. But circumstances really have played an outsize role.

There is a lesson in this reality: Whereas the type B can exist calmly and graciously in virtually any context, no matter the stress potential, the type A should perhaps consider less "provocative" environs. No one told me.

Much of the online information regarding the type A personality attributes to the type elevated blood pressure, cardiovascular disease and sleep disturbances. I take issue with this assumption and would encourage psychology professionals to reconsider their stance.

I know it may be counter-intuitive. But I suspect a type A suffers few, if any, adverse health effects. She holds nothing inside, and reserves no conflict for a later date. She strikes when the iron is hot, releasing anger and frustration in real time, for better or worse.

Worse being, of course, that the timing of her assertiveness is often not ideal. Conversely, and for the better, she keeps herself largely free of the physical manifestations of bottling up her anger – adverse effects like hypertension and insomnia.

There is one very useful aspect of my type A persona for which I have always been grateful. That is, I have never shied away from conflict.

"Ya wanna engage? No problem," has always been my mantra.

The idea is to keep the interaction positive, in the assertiveness range while avoiding escalation into aggression.

Whereas type A's need type B's, if for no other reason than to secure a calming influence, type B's need type A's to counter their conflict-averseness. A match made in heaven? It can be.

Deep down, a type A knows she needs to chill out. But under many circumstances she simply cannot. So, she flogs herself with excessive self-criticism and feelings of shame.

In that a type A can relieve some of the guilt and humiliation through self-deprecation, the type B appears to have no such need.

My type A inclinations continue to be ingrained, even if they may originally have come to fruition due to external factors. After decades of dominance, they emanate from the core of my being. They are who I am.

But having reined in my personality's worst excesses, I find I can employ my remaining type A energies toward more worthwhile and creative endeavors. A blessing!

As for my parents, now both deceased, I have forgiven them for the hurt and disappointments of the past. I know they loved me too much to have caused me intentional pain and hardship. They knew not what they'd done.

I wonder... If my childhood had been easier, would I have endured the trials from which I learned so many life lessons? Would I have achieved as many accomplishments? Would I be as strong? Would I have written, so far, two books? Would I be the person I am today?

Those will always remain questions with unknown answers.

I've learned there is no point in regret. Although we make choices while exercising our free will, it all ultimately comes down to God's plan for our time spent here on Earth. I believe there is a reason our lives travel the paths we walk. And, along the way, we'd best stay observant so as not to miss the intended takeaways.

Arguably my most significant "speed bump" was the passing of my husband Sam from cancer in 2019. But unlike so many of the other challenges I've faced, this one I mostly navigated with grace and optimism.

In a surprising turn, the potentially devastating event guided me into a remarkable next chapter of life. I was presented with unexpected insights and opportunities, which I willingly embraced. Mysterious occurrences, strongly reflecting serendipity, peppered my extraordinary existence following Sam's passing. This unforeseen and positive reality is described in detail in my book *To Sam, With Love: A Surviving Spouse's Story of Inspired Grief*, published in 2022.

Fun fact: The publication date of *To Sam, With Love*, randomly assigned by the publisher, is Sam's birthday. Serendipity? I believe so.

I still experience "speed bumps" whose effects have not diminished over a lifetime of repeat occurrences. I suspect they have to do with my impatient, and sometimes aggressive, type A style that has frequently caused me to feel inferior and unworthy.

For instance, I have almost never received flowers from a man *just because*. (A boy in high school once gave me a single red rose, which I acknowledge was very romantic. But his was a schoolboy crush and, alas, the feelings weren't mutual.)

As a type A, I perceive myself to be someone lacking sweetness. Hence, the reason for the dearth of sentimentality on the part of the men in my life? Perhaps yes, but I suspect no. I am far too hard on myself. Other type A's must surely relate.

Sam would give me beautiful flowers on our anniversary, Valentine's Day, and perhaps other special occasions. More than once, I tried to convey to him how much more the gesture would mean if it came on a random day when he happened to feel especially lucky to be my husband. But it never happened, not with Sam or anyone else.

I guess it's just one more example of how it seems I'll forever be in search of external validation. Where a more centered individual's self-worth emanates from within, mine never has. Perhaps, then, my goal for the future should be to feel whole without having to perpetually *achieve*. Therein lies the real challenge of my life. Can other type A's identify?

As *most* of my life's hardships are now relegated to the past, I wouldn't trade my experiences for anyone else's. I am satisfied, even happy, with the "road" I've taken, a course rife with "cul-de-sacs," "dead ends" and "speed bumps." In the end, they've all been blessings.

So, with immense gratitude let's raise a glass to the "speed bumps." Hear, hear…

Author's Bio

Vicki Paris Goodman was born in Los Angeles, California, and grew up near the hub of the Hollywood entertainment industry. After marrying Sam Goodman in 1997, the couple resided in Long Beach until retirement prompted a move to the mountains of central Arizona in 2016.

Ms. Goodman is a retired mechanical engineer and real estate appraiser. She sings and plays violin semi-professionally, and served a Long Beach-area newspaper as theater critic for over twenty years.

Ms. Goodman is also the author of *To Sam, With Love: A Surviving Spouse's Story of Inspired Grief.*

www.ingramcontent.com/pod-product-compliance
Lightning Source LLC
Chambersburg PA
CBHW072153070526
44585CB00015B/1121